Introduction to Market Research Using the SAS® System

Version 6
First Edition

SAS Institute Inc.
SAS Campus Drive
Cary, NC 27513

The correct bibliographic citation for this manual is as follows: SAS Institute Inc., *Introduction to Market Research Using the SAS® System*, Cary, NC: SAS Institute Inc., 1994. 180 pp.

Introduction to Market Research Using the SAS® System

Contents

Credits

Documentation

Design and Production   Design, Production, and Printing Services

Style Programming   Publications Technology Development

Technical Review   James J. Ashton, John C. Brocklebank, Ottis R. Cowper, John Green, Gerardo I. Hurtado, Martin Johnson, Kristin R. Latour, Cathy A. Maahs-Fladung, Wayne E. Watson

Writing and Editing   Brent L. Cohen, N. Elizabeth Malcom, Patricia Glasgow Moell, Josephine P. Pope, Susan E. Willard

Using This Book

Purpose

Introduction to Market Research Using the SAS System provides an introduction to several basic market research applications and contains numerous examples showing how to perform these applications with SAS software.

This book describes how to use SAS software for the following market research tasks:

□ taking random samples from a SAS data set

□ creating survey forms and managing survey data

□ writing tabular reports and producing plots, charts, and maps

□ analyzing qualitative frequency data

□ performing basic statistical analysis, including various types of regression

□ accessing database tables and files.

Audience

Introduction to Market Research Using the SAS System is written for new or intermediate-level users of SAS software who want to learn more about using SAS software for basic market research applications.

Prerequisites

The following table summarizes the SAS System concepts that you need to understand in order to use *Introduction to Market Research Using the SAS System* effectively:

You need to know how to	Refer to
invoke the SAS System at your site	instructions provided by the SAS Software Consultant at your site
use base SAS software	*SAS Language and Procedures: Introduction* for a brief introduction; or *SAS Language and Procedures: Usage* for a more thorough introduction
create and manipulate SAS data sets using the DATA step	*SAS Language: Reference*
use the SAS Text Editor to enter and edit text	*SAS Language: Reference*
manipulate SAS data sets using SAS procedures	*SAS Procedures Guide*

The following table describes the SAS System components that you should have licensed at your site in order to use *Introduction to Market Research Using the SAS System* effectively:

In order to	You should have access to
perform most of the example applications described in this book	base SAS software, SAS/FSP software, and SAS/STAT software
produce high-resolution quality graphics	SAS/GRAPH software
access database tables and files with the SAS System	SAS/ACCESS software

Organization of the Book

Introduction to Market Research Using the SAS System is divided into seven chapters and one appendix. Each is described here briefly.

Chapter 1, "Introduction"
   describes some of the marketing research applications discussed in the book.

Chapter 2, "Sampling"
   explains how to use SAS software to take random samples from a SAS data set.

Chapter 3, "Creating Survey Forms and Managing Survey Data"
   shows how to use SAS software to produce survey forms and mailing labels for surveys. It also shows how to enter the data collected from a survey and how to manage, combine, and examine data in SAS data sets.

Chapter 4, "Producing Marketing Reports"
   explains how to use various components of the SAS System to produce tabular reports, charts, plots, and maps.

Chapter 5, "Analyzing Qualitative Marketing Data"
   describes how to use SAS software to produce crosstabulation tables and perform statistical analyses for marketing data that are classified as qualitative.

Chapter 6, "Analyzing Quantitative Marketing Data"
   describes how to use SAS software to perform statistical analysis of marketing data that are classified as quantitative. These analyses include correlation, regression, and *t*-tests.

Chapter 7, "Accessing Database Tables and Files"
   introduces and provides a tutorial approach to explaining SAS/ACCESS software, which is an interface that links data stored in other vendors' database tables or files to the SAS System.

Appendix, "Sample SAS Data Sets"
   contains the full code that creates three large sample SAS data sets used in examples in the book.

Feedback

If you have comments or suggestions about this book, any other SAS software manual, or the software, we would like to hear from you. You may write us at the Institute or contact us by using one of our electronic mail addresses. Refer to the Your Turn page at the end of the book for information on how to forward your comments to the appropriate division.

Additional Documentation

SAS Institute provides many publications about products of the SAS System and how to use them on specific hosts. For a complete list of SAS publications, you should refer to the current *Publications Catalog.* The catalog is produced twice a year. You can order a free copy of the catalog by writing, calling, or faxing the Institute:

> SAS Institute Inc.
> Book Sales Department
> SAS Campus Drive
> Cary, NC 27513
> Telephone: 919-677-8000
> Fax: 919-677-8166

Additional SAS Software Documentation

The following documents provide more information about the SAS System components discussed in *Introduction to Market Research Using the SAS System*:

Base SAS Software

☐ *SAS Guide to TABULATE Processing, Second Edition* (order #A56095) explains how to produce reports in tabular format with the TABULATE procedure.

☐ *SAS Guide to the REPORT Procedure: Usage and Reference, Version 6, First Edition* (order #A56088) explains how to use PROC REPORT to customize reports in both windowing and nonwindowing environments.

☐ *SAS Language and Procedures: Introduction, Version 6, First Edition* (order #A56074) provides introductory information about base SAS software.

☐ *SAS Language and Procedures: Syntax, Version 6, First Edition* (order #A56077) provides a quick but complete reference to the syntax for portable base SAS software.

☐ *SAS Language and Procedures: Usage, Version 6, First Edition* (order #A56075) is a task-oriented usage guide that presents base SAS software features and procedures and shows users in a step-by-step format how to use the software to perform common tasks.

☐ *SAS Language and Procedures: Usage 2, Version 6, First Edition* (order #A56078) is a task-oriented usage guide that presents base SAS software features and procedures and shows users in a step-by-step format how to use the software to perform tasks of moderate difficulty for specific purposes.

□ *SAS Language: Reference, Version 6, First Edition* (order #A56076) contains complete reference information for all features of the SAS language that are not host specific, including all features that are not procedures.

□ *SAS Procedures Guide, Version 6, Third Edition* (order #A56080) provides complete reference information for all procedures in base SAS software since Release 6.06.

□ SAS Technical Report P-258, *Using the REPORT Procedure in a Nonwindowing Environment*, Release 6.07 (order #A59175) provides complete reference and usage information on the statements and options in PROC REPORT.

SAS/ACCESS Software

See the list of documents at the end of Chapter 7.

SAS/ASSIST Software

□ *Getting Started with the SAS System Using SAS/ASSIST Software, Version 6, First Edition* (order #A56085) provides a task-oriented set of instructions for using the menu-driven interface of SAS/ASSIST software to access the power of the SAS System.

SAS/ETS Software

□ *SAS/ETS User's Guide, Version 6, Second Edition* (order #A56010) provides complete reference information on the seventeen procedures in Version 6 SAS/ETS software.

□ *SAS/ETS Software: Applications Guide 1, Version 6, First Edition* (order #A56008) is a task-oriented usage guide that shows how to use SAS/ETS software for modeling and forecasting time series data, printing financial reports, and analyzing loans.

□ *SAS/ETS Software: Applications Guide 2, Version 6, First Edition* (order #A56009) is a task-oriented guide for econometricians that shows how to use SAS/ETS software for modeling, simulating, and forecasting with economic data.

SAS/FSP Software

□ *SAS/FSP Software: Usage and Reference, Version 6, First Edition* (order #A56001) provides usage and reference sections for all SAS/FSP software procedures, statements, and commands.

SAS/GRAPH Software

□ *SAS/GRAPH Software: Introduction, Version 6, First Edition* (order #A56019) introduces new SAS/GRAPH software users to producing charts, plots, maps, and text slides.

□ *SAS/GRAPH Software: Reference, Version 6, First Edition, Volume 1* and *Volume 2* (order #A56020) provide complete details for all features of SAS/GRAPH software.

□ *SAS/GRAPH Software: Syntax, Version 6, First Edition* (order #A56024) provides a quick and complete reference to the syntax for SAS/GRAPH software.

□ *SAS/GRAPH Software: Usage, Version 6, First Edition* (order #A56021) shows you in step-by-step format how to perform common graphing tasks.

SAS/QC Software

☐ *SAS/QC Software: Reference, Version 6, First Edition* (order #A5857) provides a complete reference for Version 6 SAS/QC software.

☐ *SAS/QC Software: ADX Menu System for Design of Experiments, Version 6, First Edition* (order #A56039) is an introductory guide to using the ADX menu system for constructing and analyzing designed experiments.

SAS/STAT Software

☐ *SAS/STAT User's Guide, Version 6, Fourth Edition, Volume 1* and *Volume 2* (order #A56045) provides complete reference information for all procedures in SAS/STAT software.

☐ SAS Technical Report P-229, *SAS/STAT Software: Changes and Enhancements, Release 6.07* (order #A59146) describes new procedures and new features in existing procedures that have been added to SAS/STAT software.

Chapter 1 Introduction

Market Research Tasks

Introduction to Market Research Using the SAS System provides information on various features and capabilities of SAS software that can help you perform basic market research. This book describes some of the many tasks involved in market research.

Sampling

Use the DATA step or the SQL procedure in base SAS software to select a random sample from a population of interest (contained in a SAS data set). By studying the sample, you can make inferences about the parent population from which the sample is drawn. You can also use the SAS System to compute the minimum sample size necessary to achieve a given level of confidence in your inferences about means or proportions.

Creating Survey Forms and Mailing Labels

Use the DATA step or SAS/FSP software to create customized printed survey forms. You can also use the FORMS procedure to create mailing labels for survey forms.

Entering, Managing, and Examining Survey Data

You use the DATA step and the FSEDIT or FSVIEW procedures from SAS/FSP software to enter data. An example in Chapter 3 shows how you can use PROC FSEDIT to create a customized data entry application. Use the SET, MERGE, and UPDATE statements in the DATA step, or use the APPEND procedure when you need to combine two or more SAS data sets. The SORT procedure and the UNIVARIATE procedure in base SAS software help you examine survey data for duplicate, extreme, or missing values.

Producing Reports and Graphics

You can use the SAS System to create the following types of reports and graphics:

Table 1.1
Producing Reports
and Graphics

To produce . . .	Use . . .
tabular reports	the PRINT, REPORT, and TABULATE procedures from base SAS software
plots of marketing data over time	the PLOT procedure from base SAS software or the GPLOT procedure from SAS/GRAPH software
block charts, bar charts, and pie charts	the GCHART procedure from SAS/GRAPH software
block maps and choropleth maps	the GMAP procedure from SAS/GRAPH software

Additionally, you can use the menu-driven SAS/ASSIST software to help you produce reports, charts, tables, and plots without needing to learn the syntax of the individual procedures.

Performing Statistical Analysis

The type of statistical analysis you perform on marketing data depends upon whether the data can be classified as qualitative or quantitative. The types of analysis you perform for qualitative data are typically different than the types of analysis you perform for quantitative data. To understand the distinction between the two types of data, you need to know about the four levels of data measurement.

nominal level data
> have names, and these names have no inherent ordering. An example of nominally scaled data are flavors such as sweet, salty, and sour. Another example is sex, whether it is coded as male and female, or 1 for male and 2 for female. The numbers assigned to the items have no meaning other than to associate a name with the value of the variable.

ordinal level data
> have an inherent ordering that corresponds to the values of a variable. An example of ordinal data are flavors coded as mild, medium, and strong. Only the order of the ordinal values is important, not the actual values. For example, you could assign the values 1, 2, and 3 to the three ordinally scaled flavors, or you could assign the values 100, 500, and 1000.

interval level data
> are numeric, have an inherent ordering, and the differences between values have meaning. An example of interval measurement is the temperature scale. A temperature of 25 degrees is 10 degrees warmer than a temperature of 15 degrees. Further up the scale, a temperature of 40 degrees is also 10 degrees warmer than a temperature of 30 degrees. Note, however, that you cannot say that a temperature of 40 degrees is twice as warm as a temperature of 20 degrees.

ratio level data

> are numeric, have an inherent ordering, have meaningful difference values, and have a meaningful value of zero. Another way of stating this is that the ratio of two values is interpretable. For example, money is measured on a ratio scale because the value of zero is meaningful. An item with a price of 50 dollars costs twice as much as an item with a price of 25 dollars.

Data measured at the nominal level are always qualitative. Data measured at the interval or ratio level are always quantitative, but they can be treated as if they were qualitative if the variables of interest have only a few distinct values. Data measured at the ordinal level are sometimes qualitative and sometimes quantitative. For example, if you have judgments of relative likelihood to buy a product, measured on a Likert scale of 1 to 7, you can say that the values are measured at the ordinal level. However, the ratings have some properties of interval measurement, in that the difference between the ratings of 1 and 2 may be about the same as the difference between the ratings of 2 and 3, and so on. Thus, you can treat these qualitative data as if they were quantitative. For more information on treating ordinal data as if they were measured at the interval level, see Babbie (1973).

Qualitative Data Analysis

For data that are classified as qualitative, you typically create crosstabulation tables and perform analyses based on the frequency counts in the cells of the table. You use the FREQ procedure (from base SAS software or SAS/STAT software) to produce the crosstabulation tables and perform the relevant statistical tests. A common analysis for qualitative data is the test of no association between two variables. The specific analysis depends on the size of the table (2 x 2, or larger) and whether the data have been stratified (divided into groups).

Quantitative Data Analysis

For data that have been classified as quantitative, you can perform a wide variety of inferential statistical tests:

The UNIVARIATE and CORR procedures from base SAS software compute descriptive statistics, test for normality, and compute correlations between variables.

The PLOT procedure from base SAS software and the GPLOT procedure from SAS/GRAPH software can be used to examine scatter plots of data.

The TTEST procedure from SAS/STAT software and the MEANS procedure from base SAS software produce a *t* test for comparing means from independent samples and matched samples, respectively.

The REG and LOGISTIC procedures from SAS/STAT software perform single, multiple, and logistic regression analysis. The AUTOREG procedure from SAS/ETS software performs regression analysis for time series data.

Accessing Database Tables and Files

SAS/ACCESS software enables you to have access to data stored in other vendors' database tables or files. It provides a link between the SAS System and the database tables or files.

Advanced Market Research

This book does not attempt to cover every topic in market research. It deliberately omits several methods of statistical analysis that are considered more advanced and omits complex areas of market research. However, you can still use the SAS System to perform many of these advanced market research analyses. Some of these advanced topics and the SAS procedures used to perform them include the following:

Table 1.2 *Advanced Market Research Procedures*

Topic	Procedure	Comment
conjoint analysis	the TRANSREG procedure in SAS/STAT software	can perform both metric and nonmetric conjoint analysis.
	the OPTEX and FACTEX procedures, along with the ADX menu system in SAS/QC software	can generate orthogonal designs for both main-effects models and models with interactions. PROC OPTEX and the ADX menu system can generate nonorthogonal designs, too.
correspondence analysis	the CORRESP procedure in SAS/STAT software	performs simple and multiple correspondence analysis and outputs the coordinates for plotting.
multidimensional preference analysis	the PRINQUAL procedure in SAS/STAT software	performs multidimensional preference analysis and outputs the coordinates for plotting.
multidimensional scaling	the MDS procedure in SAS/STAT software	performs multidimensional scaling.
multinomial choice modeling	the PHREG procedure in SAS/STAT software	fits multinomial choice models.
preference mapping	the TRANSREG procedure in SAS/STAT software	performs preference mapping and outputs the coordinates.

For more information on using SAS software for advanced market research, see Kuhfeld (1992).

References

□   Babbie, E.R. (1973), *Survey Research Methods*, Belmont, CA: Wadsworth.

□   Kuhfeld, W.F. (1992), "Marketing Research: Uncovering Competitive Advantages," *Proceedings of the Seventeenth Annual SAS Users Group International*, 1304-1312.

6

Chapter 2 Sampling

Introduction

Sampling is the process of selecting a subset of observations from a population of interest in order to study the sample and make inferences about the parent population from which the sample is drawn. A sample must be representative of its parent population for you to make valid inferences about the population from a study of the sample. The best way to get a representative sample from a population is to select a *random sample*. In a random sample each observation has a known (and usually nonzero) chance of inclusion in the sample. A *simple random sample* is one in which each observation in the population has an equal chance of being selected for the sample. Other types of random sampling methods use unequal probabilities to weight the chances that some observations have greater likelihood than other observations of being included in the sample.

Most questionnaires, surveys, and experiments are administered to a random sample of a given population, rather than to the entire population, because of limits on time, money, and other resources. For example, if you want to learn about the purchasing behavior of married people between the ages of 25 and 30, you cannot feasibly send a questionnaire to all of the people who fall into this population category. However, you can make accurate inferences about the behavior of the full population from the results obtained from a random sample of the population. The following statement is an example of the type of inference you can make based on the results of a questionnaire on future car purchases given to a sample of 300 people: "You can be 95% certain that between 15% to 21% of married couples between the ages of 25 and 30 making over $40,000 per year will buy a new car within the next three years." The precision and confidence that you have in your inferences about a population depend on the variability in the data and the size of the sample. In general, lower variability and larger samples increase the precision and confidence of your inferences about populations.

This chapter describes how to use the SAS System to perform common types of random sampling. It also explains how to calculate sample sizes necessary to achieve a given level of precision or confidence in your inferences about a population. For the examples in this chapter, assume that the data from which you want to sample are contained in a SAS data set.

Types of Sampling

You can perform many different types of sampling with the SAS System. The type of sampling you choose depends on the goals of your research and on the type of analysis you want to perform on the data collected from the sample. This chapter discusses the following types of sampling:

□   sampling without replacement

□   sampling with replacement

□   stratified random sampling.

A common distinction is whether the sampling is done with replacement or without replacement. In *sampling with replacement*, observations selected for the sample are returned to the parent population so that they may be selected again for the same sample. In *sampling without replacement*, observations selected for a sample are not returned to the population. Thus, they cannot be selected again for the same sample. Most sampling designs for surveys or questionnaires use sampling without replacement because having duplicate individuals or households in the same sample is not useful. When you sample with replacement, there is a chance of producing imprecise or misleading values for the statistics you compute from the sample.

Sometimes you want to take random samples from multiple subgroups or categories of a population. The categories of the population are called *strata*, and this technique is known as *stratified random sampling*. To use this method, you must know the stratifying variable for all observations, but in some cases you can obtain this information after selecting observations for a sample. Stratified sampling can increase the precision and confidence you have in your analyses if the stratifying variable is correlated with the object of your study. For example, you can divide the country into four geographical regions and give a survey about car purchases to a random sample of people within each of the regions to form a stratified random sample. Your inferences about the population will be more precise if geographic regions are somehow related to car purchases. You can decide that each strata should have equal numbers in the sample or different proportions in the full sample. For example, a sparsely populated region can make up a smaller proportion of the sample than can a more densely populated region. You use the proportions in the original population to help you decide how to assign proportions to the strata in the sample.

SAS Data Set Example

For the examples in this chapter, suppose that you want to send a survey to a sample from a population of people who have purchased a new or used car in the past eight years. You have a data set, CARINFO, containing information about the people in this population of interest. For this example, consider this dataset as the complete population of interest. The CARINFO data set contains information about each person's most recent car purchase and income level. Specifically, the CARINFO data set contains the following four variables:

IDNUM	is an identifying variable for each person in the data set. You can also use this variable to link observations in the CARINFO data set to observations in another data set containing mailing addresses.
INCOME	is a formatted numeric variable that describes each individual's income level as one of four distinct categories.
YEARPUR	is a date variable containing the most recent year in which the individual purchased a car.
TYPE	is a character variable describing whether the most recent car purchase was a new or used car.

Although you will probably work with much larger data sets, demonstrating the sampling techniques described in this chapter is easier with a relatively small data set. The CARINFO data set contains 50 observations. You can readily apply the methods described here to larger data sets.

The following PROC PRINT step lists the 50 observations from the data set CARINFO in Output 2.1:

```
proc print data=carinfo;
   title 'Car Purchase Data';
run;
```

Output 2.1
Listing of Data Set
CARINFO

```
                         Car Purchase Data

         OBS        INCOME          IDNUM    YEARPUR    TYPE

          1     $20,001 - $40,000    1001     1987      used
          2     Under $20,000        1002     1986      used
          3     $40,001 - $60,000    1003     1988      used
          4     Over $60,000         1004     1989      new
          5     Over $60,000         1005     1992      new
          6     Over $60,000         1006     1987      used
          7     $40,001 - $60,000    1007     1991      new
          8     Under $20,000        1008     1991      new
          9     Over $60,000         1009     1989      new
         10     $40,001 - $60,000    1010     1990      used
         11     Over $60,000         1011     1989      used
         12     $40,001 - $60,000    1012     1992      used
         13     Over $60,000         1013     1993      new
         14     $20,001 - $40,000    1014     1992      new
         15     $20,001 - $40,000    1015     1989      used
         16     $40,001 - $60,000    1016     1989      new
         17     $40,001 - $60,000    1017     1990      new
         18     Over $60,000         1018     1990      new
         19     Over $60,000         1019     1991      new
         20     Over $60,000         1020     1992      used
         21     Over $60,000         1021     1992      new
         22     $40,001 - $60,000    1022     1990      new
         23     Over $60,000         1023     1991      new
         24     Under $20,000        1024     1987      new
```

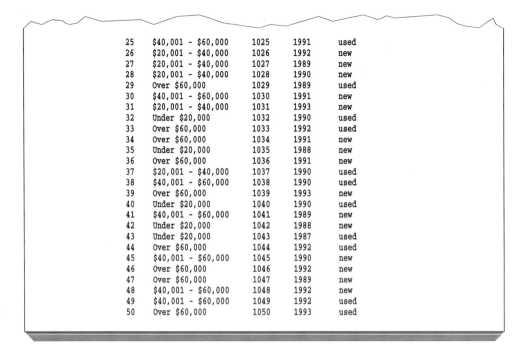

25	$40,001 - $60,000	1025	1991	used
26	$20,001 - $40,000	1026	1992	new
27	$20,001 - $40,000	1027	1989	new
28	$20,001 - $40,000	1028	1990	new
29	Over $60,000	1029	1989	used
30	$40,001 - $60,000	1030	1991	new
31	$20,001 - $40,000	1031	1993	new
32	Under $20,000	1032	1990	used
33	Over $60,000	1033	1992	used
34	Over $60,000	1034	1991	new
35	Under $20,000	1035	1988	new
36	Over $60,000	1036	1991	new
37	$20,001 - $40,000	1037	1990	used
38	$40,001 - $60,000	1038	1990	used
39	Over $60,000	1039	1993	new
40	Under $20,000	1040	1990	used
41	$40,001 - $60,000	1041	1989	new
42	Under $20,000	1042	1988	new
43	Under $20,000	1043	1987	used
44	Over $60,000	1044	1992	used
45	$40,001 - $60,000	1045	1990	new
46	Over $60,000	1046	1992	new
47	Over $60,000	1047	1989	new
48	$40,001 - $60,000	1048	1992	new
49	$40,001 - $60,000	1049	1992	used
50	Over $60,000	1050	1993	used

Calculating Sample Sizes

Before you take a random sample, you want to know how large a sample you need to achieve a given level of confidence in your inferences about the parent population. The general rule is that larger samples and smaller variability in the population enable you to make more precise inferences about the parent population with greater confidence. The size of the parent population has no bearing on the required sample size necessary for valid statistical inferences. Your approach to calculating sample size differs depending on whether you calculate a mean or a proportion for the variable of interest.

Sample Sizes for Confidence Intervals about Means

Suppose that you want to be 95% confident that the true population mean of a variable is within a specified number of units of the estimated mean you calculate from your sample. For example, you can estimate the average miles each individual in your sample drives to and from work each week. You want to be 95% confident that the population mean is within 10 miles of your estimate, that is, 10 miles higher or 10 miles lower than your estimate. In other words, you want a 95% confidence interval with a precision of 10 miles. Thus, the width of the entire confidence interval is 20 miles. The size of the sample you need to achieve 95% confidence that the population mean is within that interval depends on the variability in the data. Assuming that the distribution of the sample mean is approximately normal, the following statistical formula expresses the relationships among the size of the interval, the degree of confidence, the variability in the data, and the sample size:

$$d = \frac{z_c \sigma_x}{\sqrt{n}}$$

where d is the half width of the desired interval, z_c is the z-statistic for the desired level of confidence, σ_x is the population standard deviation, and n is the sample size.

Solving for n produces

$$n = \left[\frac{z_c \sigma_x}{d}\right]^2 \quad .$$

You usually don't know the population standard deviation (σ_x), but you can make educated guesses for it and use these guesses to calculate sample sizes. You can use several different guesses for the standard deviation to get a feel for the required sample size under different conditions. For example, if you estimate σ_x to be 15, then the required sample size for a 95% confidence interval with a half width of 10 units, or a total width of 20 units, is

$$n = \left[\frac{(1.96)15}{10}\right]^2 = 8.64 \quad .$$

Thus, you need a sample size of 9.

If you estimate σ_x to be 30, then the required sample size is

$$n = \left[\frac{(1.96)30}{10}\right]^2 = 34.57 \quad .$$

Thus, you need a sample size of 35.

The following SAS program shows how to program sample size calculations in a DATA step for various half-width intervals ranging from 5 to 15 for estimated population standard deviations ranging from 5 to 30. This SAS program calculates the sample sizes necessary to achieve 99% confidence intervals about the mean, in addition to the sample sizes for 95% confidence intervals about the mean. The results are shown in Output 2.2.

```
data sample1(drop=z95 z99);
   z95=1.96;
   z99=2.58;
   do interval=5 to 15 by 5;
      do stddev=5 to 30 by 5;
         n95=ceil((z95*stddev/interval)**2);
         n99=ceil((z99*stddev/interval)**2);
         output;
      end;
   end;
run;

proc print data=sample1;
   title 'Sample Sizes for 95% and 99% Confidence Intervals';
run;
```

Output 2.2
Sample Size
Calculations for
Means

```
                    Sample Sizes for 95% and 99% Confidence Intervals

            OBS      INTERVAL      STDDEV      N95      N99

             1          5            5          4        7
             2          5           10         16       27
             3          5           15         35       60
             4          5           20         62      107
             5          5           25         97      167
             6          5           30        139      240
             7         10            5          1        2
             8         10           10          4        7
             9         10           15          9       15
            10         10           20         16       27
            11         10           25         25       42
            12         10           30         35       60
            13         15            5          1        1
            14         15           10          2        3
            15         15           15          4        7
            16         15           20          7       12
            17         15           25         11       19
            18         15           30         16       27
```

The N95 and N99 variables contain the minimum sample size necessary for 95% and 99% confidence, respectively, that the true mean is greater or less than the estimated mean by the amount specified in the INTERVAL variable, for the given population standard deviation specified in the STDDEV variable.

Sample Sizes for Confidence Intervals about Proportions

You use a slightly different approach to determine the sample size necessary to achieve a given level of confidence that a population proportion is within a given interval. The standard deviation of a proportion, p, is expressed in the following formula where n is the sample size:

$$\sigma_p = \sqrt{p(1-p)/n} \quad .$$

Assuming that the proportion is approximately normally distributed, the formula representing the half-width of a confidence interval, d, is

$$d = z_c\sigma_p = \frac{z_c\sqrt{p(1-p)}}{\sqrt{n}} \quad .$$

Solving for n produces

$$n = \frac{z_c^2(p(1-p))}{d^2} \quad .$$

Note that the variation in p is maximized when $p = .50$. Thus, you can calculate the sample size based on a "worst-case scenario" when $p = .50$. Using $p = .50$ is a conservative approach that produces the largest possible sample sizes for a given confidence interval. If you have reasons to expect a specific proportion, for example, $p = .10$, you can calculate the sample size based on that proportion. If you use a proportion other than .50, the required sample size decreases for a given confidence interval. The further you move away from .50 (towards 0 or 1), the smaller the required sample size becomes.

For example, suppose you want to be 95% confident that the true proportion of people in your target population who intend to purchase a new car is no more than .05 greater or less than the proportion you estimated from your survey. Because you have no prior assumptions about what proportion you expect to estimate from your survey, you take the conservative approach and use $p = .50$. Use the following formula to calculate the necessary sample size for this example:

$$n = \frac{1.96^2(.5(1 - .5))}{.05^2} = 384.16 \qquad .$$

Rounding up, you see that you need a sample size of 385 to be 95% confident that the true proportion of people who intend to purchase a new car is within .05 of the proportion you estimate from your sample.

The following SAS program shows how to program sample size calculations in a DATA step for various half-width intervals ranging from .01 to .15. This SAS program calculates the sample sizes necessary to achieve 99% confidence intervals, in addition to the sample sizes for 95% confidence intervals. The results are shown in Output 2.3.

```
data sample2(drop=z95 z99);
   z95=1.96;
   z99=2.58;
   do interval=.01 to .15 by .01;
       n95=ceil(.25*(z95**2)/(interval)**2);
       n99=ceil(.25*(z99**2)/(interval)**2);
       output;
   end;
run;

proc print data=sample2;
   title 'Sample Sizes for 95% and 99% Confidence Intervals';
run;
```

Output 2.3
Sample Size
Calculations for
Proportions

```
                Sample Sizes for 95% and 99% Confidence Intervals

          OBS      INTERVAL     N95      N99

           1         0.01      9604     16641
           2         0.02      2401      4161
           3         0.03      1068      1849
           4         0.04       601      1041
           5         0.05       385       666
           6         0.06       267       463
           7         0.07       196       340
           8         0.08       151       261
           9         0.09       119       206
          10         0.10        97       167
          11         0.11        80       138
          12         0.12        67       116
          13         0.13        57        99
          14         0.14        49        85
          15         0.15        43        74
```

The N95 and N99 variables contain the minimum sample size necessary for 95% and 99% confidence, respectively, that the true proportion is greater or less than the estimated proportion by no more than the amount of the half-width interval specified in the INTERVAL variable.

Simple Random Sampling without Replacement

Simple random sampling without replacement means that an observation does not go back into the pool of possible choices once it has been selected. In these examples, an observation is included in the sample only once if it is selected. If you need a precise number of observations in your sample, take an exact-sized random sample, but if the sample size does not have to be exact, it is easier to take an approximate-sized random sample.

Taking Approximate-Sized Random Samples

Taking an approximate-sized random sample is the easier method when the size of your sample does not need to be exact. In this example, the target sample size is 12, but the actual sample contains 11 observations.

To specify a condition for randomly including observations in a sample, use a subsetting IF statement with the random number function RANUNI. The RANUNI function returns a (pseudo) random number from 0 to 1 for every observation in the large data set. A criterion for selection in your sample is, for example, that an observation's corresponding random number is less than or equal to a specified number between 0 and 1. Another criterion for selection is that an observation's corresponding random number falls within a specified range of two numbers between 0 and 1. The latter method produces a sample of approximately the same size as the first method, but with possibly different observations selected for the sample depending on which numbers you use to specify the range.

As an example, if you want to sample 100 observations from a data set of 5,000 observations, you can specify that all observations with a corresponding random number less than .02 (100/5000 = .02) should be included in your sample. Alternatively, you can specify that all observations with corresponding random numbers between .90 and .92 should be included in your sample. Both methods produce sample sizes of approximately 100, but they contain different observations.

Because the data set CARINFO has 50 observations, about 24% (12/50) of the observations should be selected to make a sample of about 12. Because the target sample size is about 24% of the size of the original data, the probability of each observation being included in the sample is .24.

```
data approx;
   set carinfo;
   if ranuni(7837599)<=.24;
```

In each iteration of the DATA step, the RANUNI function returns a random number from 0 to 1. In this example, only those observations with a corresponding number from 0 to .24 are included in the sample. With the RANUNI function, you must specify a nonnegative *seed*, or arbitrary starting point, less than 2,147,483,647. Here, a positive seed, 7,837,599, is specified with the function in order to begin generating random numbers. Every time you give this exact seed, the RANUNI function produces the same series of random numbers; therefore, the sample is the same size with the same observations. If you choose a positive seed, you can reproduce the sample by specifying the same seed. If you choose zero as the seed, the computer clock time at execution is used, which makes it difficult to replicate your sample.

The following program produces and prints the random sample of approximately 12 observations (actually 11 observations) with no repeated observations, as shown in Output 2.4:

```
data approx;
   set carinfo;
   if ranuni(7837599)<=.24;
run;

proc print data=approx;
   title 'Approximate-Sized Random Sample';
run;
```

Output 2.4
Taking an
Approximate-Sized
Random Sample

```
                   Approximate-Sized Random Sample

       OBS        INCOME          IDNUM    YEARPUR    TYPE

         1    Over $60,000         1006     1987      used
         2    $40,001 - $60,000    1007     1991      new
         3    $40,001 - $60,000    1012     1992      used
         4    $20,001 - $40,000    1015     1989      used
         5    $40,001 - $60,000    1016     1989      new
         6    Over $60,000         1020     1992      used
         7    Over $60,000         1021     1992      new
         8    Over $60,000         1023     1991      new
         9    Under $20,000        1024     1987      new
        10    $20,001 - $40,000    1026     1992      new
        11    Under $20,000        1040     1990      used
```

Taking Exact-Sized Random Samples

With the previous technique for taking a random sample, the sample size is not always exact because the chance of selecting an observation remains constant. In fact, the proportion of random numbers less than or equal to a specified number (or within a specified range of numbers) usually changes from observation to observation. However, if you need to take a sample of a specific size with no duplicate observations, you can vary the probability of observations being selected. You can vary the probability according to the number of observations needed to complete your sample and the number of observations left to read in your data set.

To define two variables to represent the number of observations needed to complete your sample and the number of observations left to read in your data set, use the RETAIN statement. In the following example, K is the number of observations needed to complete the sample. K is initialized to 12 in the RETAIN statement because the desired sample size is 12. N is the number of observations left to read in the data set. Initially, 12 observations are needed to complete the sample, and 50 observations are left to read in the data set. These values change during the selection of the sample and are retained from one iteration to the next because of the RETAIN statement.

```
data exact;
   retain k 12 n;
```

You don't need to know the total number of observations in your data set. You can initialize your variable representing the number of observations left to read by using the NOBS= option and an IF-THEN statement.

Note: When you do know the total number of observations in your data set, it is easier to initialize the variable representing the number of observations left to read by listing that value after the variable in the RETAIN statement. However, listing the value on the RETAIN statement is risky if your data set is subject to frequent changes and updates. The total number of observations in your data set may change, and you may forget to change the value listed in the RETAIN statement.

The NOBS= option creates and names a temporary variable whose value is the total number of observations in the data set. To set the variable representing the number of observations left to read in your data set equal to the total number of observations in your data set, use the automatic variable _N_ in an IF-THEN statement. Every DATA step creates an automatic variable denoted _N_. It is initially set at 1, and each time the DATA step iterates, _N_ increases by 1.

In the following example, the NOBS= option creates the variable TOTAL, which is equal to 50. On the first iteration of the DATA step, N is initialized to 50 because _N_ equals 1.

```
if _n_=1 then n=total;
set carinfo nobs=total;
```

You can randomly select observations for your sample based on a probability that varies with the number of observations needed to complete your sample and the number of observations left to read in your data set. To do this, use the RANUNI function in an IF-THEN statement followed by a DO group containing an OUTPUT statement. The criterion for selection in your sample is that an observation's corresponding random number is less than or equal to the number of observations needed to complete your sample divided by the number of observations left to read in your data set. If an observation is chosen for the sample, the OUTPUT statement immediately writes that observation to the specified

SAS data set, and the number of observations needed to complete the sample decreases by 1. The number of observations left to read in the data set decreases by 1 whether or not the observation is included in the sample.

In the following example, the arbitrary positive seed specified with the RANUNI function is 747,088,789. If the random number generated is less than or equal to K divided by N, which is initially .24, the observation is written to the data set EXACT, and K decreases by 1. N decreases by 1 at the end of each iteration.

```
if ranuni(747088789)<=k/n then
   do;
      output;
      k=k-1;
   end;
n=n-1;
```

To stop collecting observations when your sample reaches its specified size, use the STOP statement in an IF-THEN statement. When the number of observations needed to complete your sample is 0, the STOP statement stops the execution of the DATA step:

```
if k=0 then stop;
```

The following complete program produces and prints the random sample of exactly 12 individuals with no repeated observations that is shown in Output 2.5.

```
data exact(drop=k n);
   retain k 12 n;
   if _n_=1 then n=total;
   set carinfo nobs=total;
   if ranuni(747088789)<=k/n then
      do;
         output;
         k=k-1;
      end;
   n=n-1;
   if k=0 then stop;
run;

proc print data=exact;
   title 'Exact-Sized Random Sample';
run;
```

Output 2.5
Taking an
Exact-Sized Random
Sample

```
                              Exact-Sized Random Sample

              OBS        INCOME          IDNUM    YEARPUR    TYPE

               1      Over $60,000        1013     1993      new
               2      $20,001 - $40,000   1014     1992      new
               3      Over $60,000        1019     1991      new
               4      $40,001 - $60,000   1022     1990      new
               5      $20,001 - $40,000   1027     1989      new
               6      Over $60,000        1029     1989      used
               7      Over $60,000        1033     1992      used
               8      Over $60,000        1036     1991      new
               9      $20,001 - $40,000   1037     1990      used
              10      Over $60,000        1044     1992      used
              11      Over $60,000        1046     1992      new
              12      Over $60,000        1050     1993      used
```

An Alternative Method of Taking Random Samples

The method of taking random samples described in the previous section has the advantage of efficiency, as it uses a single DATA step to select the sample. However, it has the disadvantage that the observations in the population data set are not equally likely to be selected for the sample. If your data are arranged in the population data set in nonrandom order, this method can result in a nonrepresentative sample being selected in some cases. To resolve this problem, you can use a sampling method that gives every observation in the data set the same probability of being selected for the sample. The disadvantage of this method is that it is less efficient, as it uses two DATA steps and the SORT procedure.

The sampling method follows three steps:

1. The first DATA step assigns random numbers to the observations in the population data set.

2. The SORT procedure sorts the data set by the values of the random numbers.

3. The second DATA step selects the first *n* observations to create a random sample of size *n*.

The following SAS statements select a random sample of size 12 from the CARINFO data set. The EXACT2 data set containing the sample is not shown.

```
data random;
   set carinfo;
   rannums=ranuni(50169426);
run;

proc sort data=random;
   by rannums;
run;

data exact2;
   set random(obs=12);
   drop rannums;
run;
```

You can also use the SQL procedure with a DATA step to take random samples using this method. The SQL procedure enables you to assign the random numbers and sort the data in a single statement. For complete reference and usage information on the SQL procedure, see the *SAS Guide to the SQL Procedure.*

The SAS statements shown below use the SQL procedure and a DATA step to select a random sample of size 12 from the CARINFO data set. The EXACT3 data set containing the sample is not shown.

```
proc sql;
    create table random as select *, (ranuni(50169426)) as rannums
            from carinfo order by rannums;
run;

data exact3;
    set random(obs=12);
    drop rannums;
run;
```

Simple Random Sampling with Replacement

Sampling with replacement means that a selected observation goes back into the pool of possible choices once it has been selected. Thus, you can select the same observation more than once for a given sample. For example, when sampling with replacement from a population of 100 items, the probability is approximately 50% that you will have duplicate observations in a sample of size 12. As the size of the population increases relative to the size of the sample, the chance of any observation being included more than once decreases, however. When the ratio of the sample size to the population size is small (for example, when the ratio is less than 0.05), sampling with replacement can be the easiest and most economical (in terms of CPU) method of sampling, as the chances of selecting duplicate observations in your sample will be low.

To randomly select observations by their observation number in your data set, use the POINT= option. The POINT= option names a variable whose value is the number of the observation that the SET statement reads. Instead of reading through the data set sequentially, a SET statement with the POINT= option reads observations directly.

▶ *Caution* . . . . *The POINT= option will not work under certain conditions.*
You cannot use the POINT= option with transport format data sets, compressed data sets, data sets in sequential format on tape or disk, or SAS/ACCESS views or the SQL procedure views that read data from external files. ▲

In this example, the variable CHOICE, calculated using the CEIL function and the RANUNI function, contains the observation number in each iteration of the individual chosen for the sample.

```
data replace;
    choice=ceil(ranuni(36830)*n);
    set carinfo point=choice nobs=n;
```

To define the variable that specifies the observation number, multiply the RANUNI function by the number of observations in your data set, and round this product up to the nearest whole number. The variable that represents the total number of observations in your data set is defined in the NOBS= option. To round up to the nearest whole number, use the CEIL function. With each iteration of the DATA step, the RANUNI function generates a random number from 0 to 1. Then, this number is multiplied by N, the total number of observations in the data set. Next, the number is rounded up to the nearest whole number to produce a random number between 1 and 50. You assign this value to the POINT= option in the SET statement to specify which of the observations, numbered 1 through 50, is chosen for the sample.

In general, if you need to generate a random number that is equally likely to fall in intervals of equal length anywhere between two points, multiply the RANUNI function by the difference between the endpoints and add the smaller endpoint. For example, to generate a random number between 30 and 50, multiply the RANUNI function by 20 and add 30. This evenly spread distribution where equal intervals are equally likely is called the *uniform distribution.* The SAS System can also generate random numbers from several other distributions. See Chapter 11, "SAS Functions," in *SAS Language: Reference* for a complete list of random number generators available in SAS software.

To specify the number of observations in your sample, you establish a counter and use the STOP statement in an IF-THEN statement. The STOP statement must be used with the POINT= option to stop the execution of the DATA step. In the following example, the variable I counts the number of observations selected for the sample because it starts at 0 and increases by 1 with each iteration of the DATA step. When the sample reaches 12 observations, the selection stops.

```
i+1;
if i > 12 then stop;
```

The following complete program produces and prints the random sample of 12 individuals with replacement that is shown in Output 2.6. Note that the observation with IDNUM=1033 has been selected twice in this sample.

```
data replace(drop=i);
    choice=ceil(ranuni(36830)*n);
    set carinfo point=choice nobs=n;
    i+1;
    if i > 12 then stop;
run;

proc print data=replace;
    title 'Random Sample with Replacement';
run;
```

Output 2.6
Taking a Random
Sample with
Replacement

```
                    Random Sample with Replacement

      OBS        INCOME          IDNUM    YEARPUR   TYPE

       1     Over $60,000         1009     1989     new
       2     Over $60,000         1019     1991     new
       3     $20,001 - $40,000    1027     1989     new
       4     Over $60,000         1033     1992     used
       5     Under $20,000        1032     1990     used
       6     $40,001 - $60,000    1025     1991     used
       7     Over $60,000         1047     1989     new
       8     Over $60,000         1011     1989     used
       9     Over $60,000         1046     1992     new
      10     Over $60,000         1033     1992     used
      11     $20,001 - $40,000    1026     1992     new
      12     Under $20,000        1008     1991     new
```

Stratified Random Sampling

The following two sections show two methods of taking stratified random samples. The first method shows the specific case of equal category representation, and the second method shows the general case where you want a different number of observations from each category to include in your sample. Both are examples of sampling without replacement.

Stratified Random Sampling of Equal-Sized Groups

If you want the same number of observations from each category included in your sample, it is easier to use this method to take a stratified random sample. This sample of 12 observations consists of three individuals from each of the four income groups. Because the process involves choosing a small sample from each of the subgroups of the data to make the entire random sample, you need to do the following:

- □ count the observations in each category

- □ sort the observations into categories

- □ combine the sorted data set with the category counts

- □ select the observations for the sample.

Count the Observations

To count the number of observations in each category, use the FREQ procedure. The following PROC FREQ step, with a TABLES statement and the OUT= option, counts the number of observations in each INCOME category and writes this information to an output SAS data set. To specify the input data set, use the DATA= option in the PROC FREQ statement. If this option is omitted, the FREQ procedure uses the most recently created SAS data set.

```
proc freq data=carinfo;
   tables income / out=bycount noprint;
run;
```

To specify the variable whose values identify the categories of observations, use the TABLES statement. In this example, the values 1, 2, 3, and 4 of the INCOME variable identify the categories of observations. Recall that these values have been formatted to represent four different income levels. To create an output SAS data set containing the variable values, frequency counts, and percentages, use the OUT= option. This data set contains a variable with the same name as the variable listed in the TABLES statement, a variable called COUNT, and a variable called PERCENT. In this example, the output SAS data set is named BYCOUNT.

Sort the Observations

To sort the observations into categories, use the SORT procedure with the BY statement. The BY statement specifies the variables whose values identify the categories of the data. The following PROC SORT step sorts the observations in the data set CARINFO into categories based on the values of the INCOME variable. To specify the input data set, use the DATA= option in the PROC SORT statement. If you omit this option, the SORT procedure uses the most recently created SAS data set.

```
proc sort data=carinfo;
   by income;
run;
```

Combine the Data Sets

To combine your sorted data set with the observation counts by category, use the MERGE statement and the BY statement in a DATA step. The MERGE statement joins corresponding observations from SAS data sets into single observations in a new SAS data set. The BY statement names the variable by which the data sets are sorted. The following MERGE statement combines the newly created data set, BYCOUNT, with the sorted list of individuals:

```
data strat1;
   merge carinfo bycount;
   by income;
```

Select the Observations

To randomly select the observations for your sample, start by using the RETAIN statement with the variable that specifies the number of observations from a category needed to complete the subsample from that category. In the following example, the variable K is the number of observations from a value of INCOME needed to complete the subsample from that value of INCOME:

```
retain k;
```

To initialize this variable for each category, use FIRST.*variable*. In the DATA step, the SAS System identifies the beginning and end of each BY group by creating the temporary variables FIRST.*variable* and LAST.*variable* for the BY variable. In the following example, when the DATA step reads the first observation from an INCOME category, K is set to 3:

```
if first.income then k=3;
```

To select the observations for your sample, use the RANUNI function to randomly choose the specified number of observations from each category. The variable COUNT, the total number of observations in a category, is written in the output data set of the PROC FREQ step. To set COUNT equal to the number of observations in a category left to read, decrease COUNT by 1 with each iteration of the DATA step. The following code is explained in detail earlier in this chapter in "Taking Exact-Sized Random Samples":

```
if ranuni(628825275)<=k/count then
   do;
       output;
       k=k-1;
   end;
count=count-1;
```

The following complete program produces and prints the stratified random sample of twelve individuals, consisting of three from each income group. The results are shown in Output 2.7.

```
proc freq data=carinfo;
   tables income / out=bycount noprint;
run;

proc sort data=carinfo;
   by income;
run;

data strat1(drop=k count);
   merge carinfo bycount(drop=percent);
   by income;
   retain k;
   if first.income then k=3;
   if ranuni(628825275)<=k/count then
      do;
          output;
          k=k-1;
      end;
   count=count-1;
run;

proc print data=bycount;
   title 'Count of Individuals by Income Group';
run;

proc print data=strat1;
   title 'Stratified Random Sample of Equal-Sized Groups';
run;
```

Output 2.7
Taking a Stratified
Random Sample of
Equal-Sized Groups

```
            Count of Individuals by Income Group              1

        OBS       INCOME          COUNT     PERCENT

         1     Under $20,000        8         16
         2     $20,001 - $40,000    8         16
         3     $40,001 - $60,000   14         28
         4     Over $60,000        20         40
```

```
          Stratified Random Sample of Equal-Sized Groups              2

     OBS      INCOME          IDNUM    YEARPUR    TYPE

      1    Under $20,000       1008     1991      new
      2    Under $20,000       1024     1987      new
      3    Under $20,000       1040     1990      used
      4    $20,001 - $40,000   1001     1987      used
      5    $20,001 - $40,000   1014     1992      new
      6    $20,001 - $40,000   1027     1989      new
      7    $40,001 - $60,000   1010     1990      used
      8    $40,001 - $60,000   1038     1990      used
      9    $40,001 - $60,000   1049     1992      used
     10    Over $60,000        1011     1989      used
     11    Over $60,000        1013     1993      new
     12    Over $60,000        1047     1989      new
```

Stratified Random Sampling of Unequal-Sized Groups

If you need to specify different numbers of observations from different categories to include in your sample, you can use this method of taking a stratified random sample. This example takes a stratified random sample that is roughly proportional to the size of the groups by income level. To take a stratified random sample of unequal-sized groups, do the following:

□ sort the observations into categories

□ specify the number of observations to select from each category

□ combine the sorted data set with the category counts

□ select the observations for the sample.

Sort the Observations

To sort the observations into categories, use the SORT procedure. The following PROC SORT step sorts the observations into categories based on the values of the variable INCOME:

```
proc sort data=carinfo;
   by income;
run;
```

Specify the Number of Observations

To specify the number of observations to select from each category, create a SAS data set with variables containing the following:

□ the values of the variable that identify the categories of observations

□ the number of observations in each category

□ the number of observations to select from each category.

To process only the variable whose values identify the categories of observations, use the KEEP= option with the SET statement. The BY statement names the variable by which the data set is sorted. The following DATA step creates a SAS data set, NSELECT, which combines the total number of observations in each INCOME category and the number of observations to select from each INCOME category:

```
data nselect;
   set carinfo(keep=income);
   by income;
```

To count the number of observations in each category, you establish a counter and use LAST.*variable.* In this example, N starts at 0 and increases by 1 with each iteration of the DATA step until it counts the number of observations in an INCOME category. To specify the number of observations to select from each category, use a CARDS statement. To write the numbers of observations in your categories and the numbers of observations to select from your categories to the new data set, use LAST.*variable* in a subsetting IF statement. In the following example, if an observation is the last in an INCOME category, K and N are written to the data set NSELECT, and N is reset to 0:

```
   n+1;
   if last.income;
   input k;
   output;
   n=0;
   cards;
2
2
3
5
;
```

When specifying the numbers of observations to select from your categories, list the numbers in order of the variable values that identify your categories. In this example, 2 individuals are selected from each of the first two income-level groups, 3 are selected from the third income-level group, and 5 are selected from the fourth income-level group.

Specifying a Fixed Proportion from Each Category

In the special case of selecting an equal proportion of observations from each category, omit the INPUT and CARDS statements and data lines. To specify the same proportion for all categories, define the variable that represents the number of observations to select from a category in an assignment statement following the subsetting IF statement. That variable should be set equal to value from the CEIL function with the argument of the product of the fixed proportion and the variable that represents the number of observations in that category. The CEIL function returns the smallest integer greater than or equal to the argument. In this example, K is set equal to CEIL(N*.25) if the desired sample contains one fourth of the people in each income group.

Combine the Data Sets

To combine the sorted observations with the category counts, use the MERGE statement and the BY statement. The following MERGE statement combines the newly created data set, NSELECT, with the sorted list of customers:

```
data strat2;
   merge carinfo nselect;
   by income;
```

Select the Observations

To select the observations for the sample, use the RANUNI function to randomly choose the specified numbers of observations from the categories. In this example, K is the number of observations from a value of INCOME needed to complete the subsample from that value of INCOME, and N is the number of observations from a value of INCOME left to read. The following code is explained in detail earlier in this chapter in "Taking Exact-Sized Random Samples":

```
if ranuni(332516)<=k/n then
   do;
      output;
      k=k-1;
   end;
n=n-1;
```

The following complete program produces and prints the stratified random sample of individuals from the four income groups that is shown in Output 2.8.

```
proc sort data=carinfo;
   by income;
run;

data nselect;
   set carinfo(keep=income);
   by income;
   n+1;
   if last.income;
   input k;
   output;
   n=0;
   cards;
2
2
3
5
;
```

```
data strat2(drop=k n);
    merge carinfo nselect;
    by income;
    if ranuni(332516)<=k/n then
        do;
            output;
            k=k-1;
        end;
    n=n-1;
run;

proc print data=nselect;
    title 'Count of Individuals by Income Level';
run;

proc print data=strat2;
    title 'Stratified Random Sample of Unequal-Sized Groups';
run;
```

Output 2.8
Taking a Stratified Random Sample of Unequal-Sized Groups

```
                    Count of Individuals by Income Level                    1

        OBS          INCOME           N    K

         1     Under $20,000          8    2
         2     $20,001 - $40,000      8    2
         3     $40,001 - $60,000     14    3
         4     Over $60,000          20    5
```

```
            Stratified Random Sample of Unequal-Sized Groups          2

        OBS          INCOME          IDNUM    YEARPUR    TYPE

         1     Under $20,000          1002     1986      used
         2     Under $20,000          1008     1991      new
         3     $20,001 - $40,000      1026     1992      new
         4     $20,001 - $40,000      1037     1990      used
         5     $40,001 - $60,000      1022     1990      new
         6     $40,001 - $60,000      1025     1991      used
         7     $40,001 - $60,000      1049     1992      used
         8     Over $60,000           1009     1989      new
         9     Over $60,000           1019     1991      new
        10     Over $60,000           1020     1992      used
        11     Over $60,000           1021     1992      new
        12     Over $60,000           1046     1992      new
```

Learning More

□   For more information on using the RANUNI function and other random number functions in SAS software, see the following:

□   Chapter 11, "SAS Functions," in *SAS Language: Reference, Version 6, First Edition*

□   Clark, M.R. and Woodward, D.E. (1992), "Generating Random Numbers with Base SAS Software," in *Observations": The Technical Journal for SAS® Software Users*, **1**, (4), 12-19.

□   For complete reference information on the FREQ, SORT, and SQL procedures, see the *SAS Procedures Guide, Version 6, Third Edition.*

□   For reference and usage information on the SQL procedure, see the *SAS Guide to the SQL Procedure: Usage and Reference, Version 6, First Edition.*

Chapter **3** Creating Survey Forms and Managing Survey Data

Introduction

This chapter shows how to use features of the SAS System to perform several tasks relating to surveys and survey data:

    ☐   create printed survey forms

    ☐   produce mailing labels

    ☐   enter data collected from surveys into SAS data sets

    ☐   create customized data entry applications

    ☐   combine SAS data sets

    ☐   examine data in SAS data sets.

Creating Printed Survey Forms with the DATA Step

The DATA step gives you precise control over the placement of text in output files. You can design the output by writing data values and character strings in particular columns and lines of an output file.

You use a PUT statement in a DATA step to write text. Specify FILE PRINT before any PUT statements in the DATA step to write your text to the procedure output file, the same place the SAS System writes output from procedures. You can specify other destinations for your text by specifying an output file in the FILE statement before the PRINT option.

In many cases, when you use a DATA step to write text to an output file, you don't need to create a new SAS data set at the same time. The special data set name _NULL_ increases program efficiency considerably by causing the DATA step to proceed as usual but without outputting observations to a data set.

The following SAS program shows how to use the PUT and FILE statements with the DATA _NULL_ specification to create an output file that contains some survey questions of interest. The following list describes the pointer controls used in this example:

□ The #*n* symbol is a line-pointer control; it tells the SAS System to move to line *n*. In this example, the pointer moves to line 3, and the PUT statement writes text on that line.

□ The @*n* symbol is a column-pointer control; it tells the SAS System to move to column *n*. In this example, the pointer moves to several different specified columns, and the PUT statement writes the text string immediately following the column-pointer control at that location.

□ The slash (/) is a pointer control that moves the pointer to the beginning of the next line. Two slashes cause the pointer to skip two lines, three slashes cause the pointer to skip three lines, and so on.

The following DATA step uses a single PUT statement to create the short survey form shown in Output 3.1:

```
data _null_;
   file print;
   put #3 @20 'CAR PURCHASE SURVEY' //
       @6 'Do you plan to purchase a new or used car' /
       @6 'within the next three years?'
       @53 'Yes' @60 'No' ///
       @6 'Assuming you need to buy a car today:' ///
       @11 'Would you prefer to buy it new or used?'
       @53 'New' @60 'Used' //
       @11 'What is the maximum amount you would be' /
       @11 'willing to spend on this car purchase?'
       @53 '_____';
run;
```

Output 3.1
A Survey Created
with a PUT
Statement in a
DATA Step

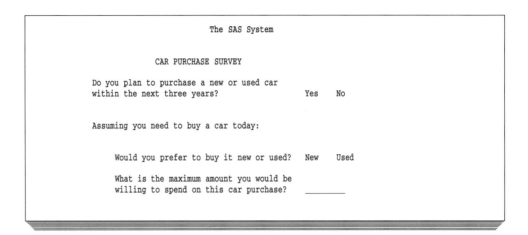

```
                              The SAS System


                    CAR PURCHASE SURVEY

          Do you plan to purchase a new or used car
          within the next three years?                    Yes    No


          Assuming you need to buy a car today:


               Would you prefer to buy it new or used?    New    Used

               What is the maximum amount you would be
               willing to spend on this car purchase?      _____
```

Now that you have created the survey form in the output file, you can print the file and make as many copies as you need. The next section shows how you can produce mailing labels for your survey forms.

Producing Mailing Labels

This section describes how to use the FORMS procedure to produce mailing labels for a continuous-feed form. Before printing the labels, you can preview them in an output file to check for errors or make changes.

Suppose you have an input file containing the names and addresses of your survey recipients. The input file looks like this:

```
Johnson, Lee. R.       P. O. Box 243       Montgomery,    AL  36113
Abbott, Brenda K.      568 Trillion Ct.    Denver,        CO  80237
Rodriguez, Juan        619 Powell Dr.      Charleston,    SC  29412
Stevenson, Mary K.     22 Meredith Blvd.   Austin,        TX  78702
Hawks, Patrick E.      Rt. 1, Box 523      Taylorsville,  NC  28681
Lee, Chen              123 Maple St.       Raleigh,       NC  27606
Weinstein, Joseph M.   Rt. 4, Box 466      Dixon,         IL  61021
Baskowski, Bonnie G.   P. O. Box 42        Sacramento,    CA  95841
```

You can enter this input file into a SAS data set using the following DATA step:

```
data labels;
   infile 'your-input-file';
   input name   $ 1-20
         street $ 22-42
         city   $ 44-59
         state  $ 60-61
         zip    $ 64-68;
run;
```

Now, use the following SAS statements and options to create the mailing labels and preview them in your default output file. For more information on using the FORMS procedure, see Chapter 26, "Producing Mailing Labels and Other Continuous-Feed Forms," in *SAS Language and Procedures: Usage, Version 6, First Edition* and the *SAS Procedures Guide, Version 6, Third Edition.*

PROC FORMS statement

> invokes the FORMS procedure and enables you to specify options about the procedure. The DATA= option specifies the input data set containing the names and addresses to print on the mailing labels. To route the output to an external file for printing, use the FILE= option to specify an external file that you have defined in a FILENAME statement.

LINE statement

> specifies what variable values from the input data set are to be printed on the specified line number of the mailing label. In this example, the values of the NAME variable are printed on line 1, the values of the STREET variable are printed on line 2, and the values of the CITY, STATE, and ZIP variables are printed on line 3.

LASTNAME option

> looks for a comma in character variables in a given LINE statement. If a comma is found, the words that appear before the comma are switched with the words that appear after the comma, and the comma is dropped. In this example, the LASTNAME option causes the NAME variable to be printed in the form FIRSTNAME INITIAL. LASTNAME.

PACK option

> removes extra blanks between variable values printed on the mailing labels. In this example, the PACK option removes any extra blanks between the CITY and STATE variables that occur due to reserving 21 spaces for the variable CITY when the data set was created.

The following SAS program produces the mailing labels shown in Output 3.2:

```
proc forms data=labels;
    line 1 name / lastname;
    line 2 street;
    line 3 city state zip / pack;
run;
```

Output 3.2
Mailing Labels
Produced with
PROC FORMS

```
                                    The SAS System

        Lee. R. Johnson
        P. O. Box 243
        Montgomery, AL 36113

        Brenda K. Abbott
        568 Trillion Ct.
        Denver, CO 80237

        Juan Rodriguez
        619 Powell Dr.
        Charleston, SC 29412

        Mary K. Stevenson
        22 Meredith Blvd.
        Austin, TX 78702

        Patrick E. Hawks
        Rt. 1, Box 523
        Taylorsville, NC 28681

        Chen Lee
        123 Maple St.
        Raleigh, NC 27606

        Joseph M. Weinstein
        Rt. 4, Box 466
        Dixon, IL 61021
```

```
Bonnie G. Baskowski
P. O. Box 42
Sacramento, CA 95841
```

Entering Data

You must first enter your survey data into a SAS data set before you can use the SAS System to examine, manipulate, or analyze the data.[*] Two basic methods of data entry in the SAS System are the DATA step and the FSEDIT or FSVIEW procedures of SAS/FSP software.

Using the DATA Step for Data Entry

Suppose you have given the survey shown in Output 3.1 to a random sample of people and collected data from 12 respondents. In reality, you would probably use a much larger sample, but this example uses a small sample for demonstration purposes. Suppose you have a file containing your raw survey data that appears as follows:

```
1013 0 1 20000
1014 0 0 12000
1019 0 0 10000
1022 1 0 7000
1027 0 1 100
1029 1 1 18000
1033 0 0 .
1036 0 1 18000
1037 1 1 16000
1044 0 1 12000
1046 0 0 8000
1050 1 0 10000
```

The first column of data contains the identification number for each respondent, and the other three columns contain the respondents' answers to questions 1, 2, and 3, in that order. Your raw data may not be as neatly arranged as the data in this example. For more information on reading raw data, see Part 2, "Reading Raw Data," in *SAS Language and Procedures, Usage 2.*

---

[*] See Chapter 7, "Accessing Database Tables and Files," for information on linking the SAS System to data that are not stored in SAS data sets.

You enter these data into the following variables in a new SAS data set called SURVEY1:

IDNUM	is the identifier variable for each respondent.
Q1	is the response to question 1 of the survey formatted as 1='Yes' and 0='No'.
Q2	is the response to question 2 of the survey formatted as 1='New' and 0='Used'.
Q3	is the response to question 3 of the survey formatted with the DOLLAR12.2 SAS format.

The SAS statements described in the following list and shown in the code sample that follows use the FORMAT procedure and the DATA step to enter the data from your survey into the SURVEY1 data set:

PROC FORMAT statement
  invokes the FORMAT procedure.

VALUE statements
  name and define formats that write a variable's value as a different value. In this example, the first VALUE statement defines the Q1FMT format, and the second VALUE statement defines the Q2FMT format. You don't need to follow the format names with a period when you define them in a VALUE statement.

FORMAT statement
  associates formats with the appropriate variables. A period follows the user-defined formats associated with the Q1 and Q2 variables in the FORMAT statement. No period follows the DOLLAR12.2 SAS format associated with the Q3 variable.

INFILE statement
  tells the SAS System where to find your raw data file.

```
proc format;
   value q1fmt 1='Yes' 0='No';
   value q2fmt 1='New' 0='Used';
run;

data survey1;
   format q1 q1fmt.
          q2 q2fmt.
          q3 dollar12.2;
   infile 'your-input-file';
   input idnum $ q1 q2 q3;
run;
```

Instead of using the INFILE statement to enter the data from your input file, you can use a CARDS statement to indicate that the raw data lines follow immediately, as shown in the following example:

```
data survey1;
   format q1 q1fmt.
          q2 q2fmt.
          q3 dollar12.2;
```

```
    input idnum $ q1 q2 q3;
cards;
1013 0 1 20000
1014 0 0 12000
1019 0 0 10000
1022 1 0 7000
1027 0 1 100
1029 1 1 18000
1033 0 0 .
1036 0 1 18000
1037 1 1 16000
1044 0 1 12000
1046 0 0 8000
1050 1 0 10000
;
```

You can use either the INFILE statement or the CARDS statement to create SAS data sets, depending on where your raw data are stored and how you prefer to enter the data. The following PRINT procedure step lists the SURVEY1 data set in Output 3.3. The VAR statement causes PROC PRINT to display the variables in the order listed; otherwise, IDNUM would be displayed last.

```
proc print data=survey1;
   var idnum q1 q2 q3;
   title 'SURVEY1 Data Set';
run;
```

Output 3.3
Survey Data Entered
with a DATA Step

```
                       SURVEY1 Data Set

          OBS   IDNUM   Q1    Q2        Q3

           1    1013    No    New    $20,000.00
           2    1014    No    Used   $12,000.00
           3    1019    No    Used   $10,000.00
           4    1022    Yes   Used    $7,000.00
           5    1027    No    New       $100.00
           6    1029    Yes   New    $18,000.00
           7    1033    No    Used         .
           8    1036    No    New    $18,000.00
           9    1037    Yes   New    $16,000.00
          10    1044    No    New    $12,000.00
          11    1046    No    Used    $8,000.00
          12    1050    Yes   Used   $10,000.00
```

Using SAS/FSP Software for Data Entry

As an alternative to using the DATA step to enter your survey data, you can use SAS/FSP to enter and update survey data. SAS/FSP gives you an interactive data-entry facility and provides you with the opportunity to build a customized end-user application. You can use the FSEDIT or FSVIEW procedures in SAS/FSP for interactive data entry. PROC FSVIEW enables editing on multiple observations at a time in a row-and-column format. PROC FSEDIT enables editing on a single observation at a time. PROC FSVIEW also enables you to specify the control level for editing. The *control level* is the degree to which the procedure can restrict access to the data set. See *SAS/FSP Software: Usage and Reference* for more information on creating and editing SAS data sets with SAS/FSP and for more information on creating customized applications.

Using the FSEDIT Procedure

To create a new SAS data set with PROC FSEDIT, use the NEW= option in the PROC FSEDIT statement. The following example SAS statements show how to create a new SAS data set called SURVEY1:

```
proc fsedit new=survey1;
run;
```

The previous statements open a blank FSEDIT New window, as shown in Display 3.1.

Display 3.1
The FSEDIT New Window

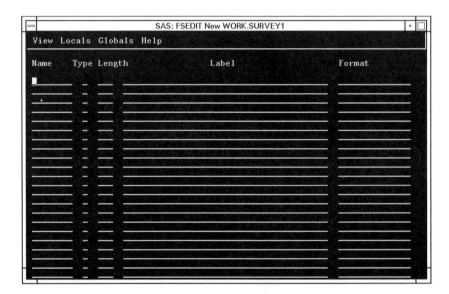

You define the structure of the new data set by describing your variables in the fields of the FSEDIT New window. You must specify a name for each variable. You can also specify a type, length, label, format, and informat. The informat field is not visible in Display 3.1, but you can scroll right to see it on your screen. By default, PROC FSEDIT specifies that all new variables are numeric with a length of 8.

Display 3.2 shows definitions for the four variables in the SURVEY1 data set. The **N** in the **Type** field indicates a numeric variable, and the dollar sign (**$**) indicates a character variable.

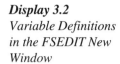

Display 3.2
*Variable Definitions
in the FSEDIT New
Window*

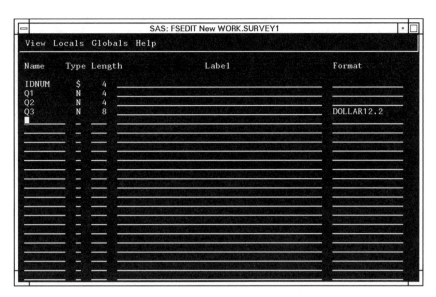

Issue the END command from the command line or select **End** from the **View** menu to close the FSEDIT New window and create the SAS data set.

Note: You cannot return to the FSEDIT New window after you close it.

When you close the FSEDIT New window, the FSEDIT window opens, which enables you to add observations and enter values to the data set. You can also open the FSEDIT window by submitting the following SAS statements:

```
proc fsedit data=survey1;
run;
```

To add observations to the data set, select **Add new record** from the **Edit** menu or issue the ADD command from a command line. Display 3.3 shows the FSEDIT window after you have typed in the first observation.

Display 3.3
FSEDIT Window
after Typing One
Observation

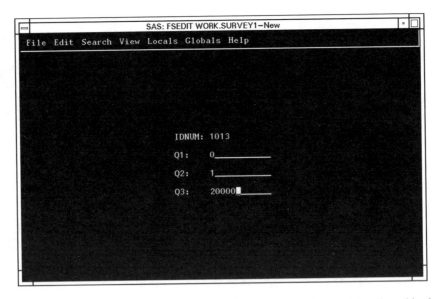

When you press ENTER, values for character variables are left-aligned in the field, values for numeric variables are right-aligned, and variables with assigned formats, such as Q3 in this example, are displayed with the specified formats. Display 3.4 shows the FSEDIT window after you press ENTER.

Display 3.4
FSEDIT Window
after Pressing
ENTER

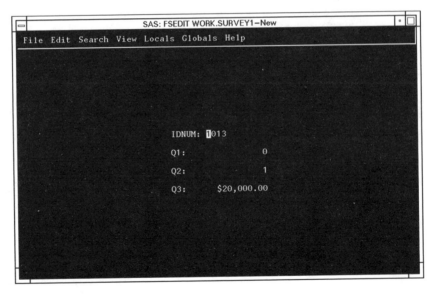

After entering your observations, select **End** from the **File** menu, or issue the END command from a command line to save the data set and end the FSEDIT session.

Using the FSVIEW Procedure

To create a new SAS data set, use the NEW= option in the PROC FSVIEW statement. The following example SAS statements show how to create a new SAS data set called SURVEY1 with PROC FSVIEW:

```
proc fsview new=survey1;
run;
```

The previous statements open a blank FSVIEW New window, which is practically identical to the FSEDIT New window shown in Display 3.1. You define your variables in the FSVIEW New Window in the same way that you define them in the PROC FSEDIT New window, as shown in Display 3.2.

Issue the END command from the command line, or select **End** from the **View** menu to close the FSVIEW New window and create the SAS data set.

Note: You cannot return to the FSVIEW New window after you close it.

When you close the FSVIEW New window, the FSVIEW window opens, which enables you to add observations to the data set and enter values. You can also open the FSVIEW window by submitting the following SAS statements:

```
proc fsview data=survey1 edit;
run;
```

To add observations to the data set, select **Autoadd** from the **Edit** menu or issue the AUTOADD command from a command line. Display 3.5 shows the FSVIEW window after you have typed in the 12 observations in your sample.

Display 3.5
FSVIEW Window
after Entering Data

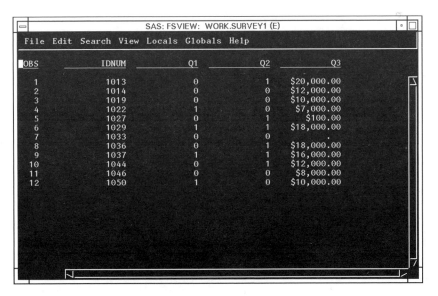

To save the data set and end the FSVIEW session, select **End** from the **File** menu, or issue the END command from a command line.

Creating a Customized Data Entry Application

You can create a customized data entry application using the FSEDIT procedure in SAS/FSP. An advantage to using a customized data entry application is that it simplifies data entry and minimizes the potential for errors in data entry.

To begin this example, initiate the FSEDIT procedure using the SCREEN= option in the PROC FSEDIT statement:

```
proc fsedit data=survey1
            screen=master.display.carsurv.screen;
run;
```

The example data set, SURVEY1, was created earlier in this chapter.

The SCREEN= option specifies the catalog and catalog entry in which information about the FSEDIT application is stored:

□   MASTER is a libref that you have assigned to a permanent SAS data library.

□   MASTER.DISPLAY is the name of the SAS catalog.

□   CARSURV.SCREEN is the name of the catalog entry.

The PROC FSEDIT statement opens the FSEDIT window by default. For the SURVEY1 data, the FSEDIT window appears, as shown in Display 3.3. To modify this display, select **Modify screen** from the **Locals** menu or issue the MODIFY command from a command line.

Note: When you use the menu to modify the display, a small window appears that prompts you for an optional password.

Next, the FSEDIT Menu window appears, as shown in Display 3.6.

Display 3.6
FSEDIT Menu
Window

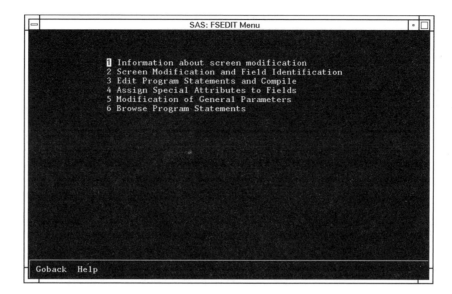

Select option 2, `Screen Modification and Field Identification`, to begin customizing the screen. This opens the FSEDIT Modify window, which enables you to use the SAS text editor to make changes to the display. (See Chapter 19, "SAS Text Editor Commands," in *SAS Language: Reference* for more information.) The initial display appears as shown in Display 3.7.

Display 3.7
Initial FSEDIT
Modify Window

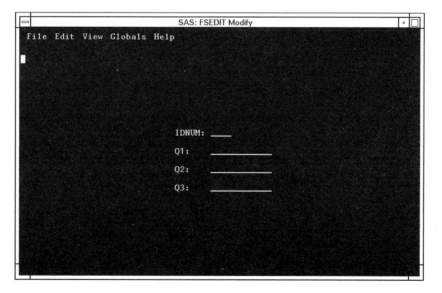

You can write over any part of the display, including variable names and the underscores that indicate variable fields.

Display 3.8 shows a redesigned data entry screen for the SURVEY1 data set. Note that this display is very similar to the survey form you created with the DATA step in Output 3.1. In fact, you could print this display to create a printed survey form. Also, you could have survey respondents enter data directly into this application.

Display 3.8
Redesigned Data
Entry Screen for
SURVEY1 Data Set

```
┌──────────────────────────────────────────────────────────────────┐
│ ═                      SAS: FSEDIT Modify                     ▫ □  │
│                                                                    │
│   File  Edit  View  Globals  Help                                  │
│                                                                    │
│                        CAR PURCHASE SURVEY                         │
│                                                   #: █▁            │
│                                                                    │
│                                                                    │
│   Do you plan to purchase a new or used car                        │
│      within the next three years?    (1=Yes 0=No)   ▁              │
│                                                                    │
│   Assuming you need to buy a car today:                            │
│                                                                    │
│      Would you prefer to buy it new or used?                       │
│                              (1=New 0=Used)   ▁                    │
│                                                                    │
│      What is the maximum amount you would be                       │
│      willing to spend on this car purchase? (in $)  ▁▁▁▁▁▁▁        │
│                                                                    │
└──────────────────────────────────────────────────────────────────┘
```

Follow these steps to produce the new display:

1. Select **Numbers** from the **Options** menu from the **Edit** menu, or issue the NUMS ON command from the command line to turn on line numbers.

2. Use the I line command to create more spaces between the variables.

3. Delete all but one underscore for the Q1 and Q2 variables.

4. Type the new label for each variable. Note that **#:** is the new label for the IDNUM variable.

5. Move to the top of the display and type in the title.

6. Use the D line command to delete lines between the title and the first variable.

7. Turn off the line numbers by selecting the **Numbers** item again or by issuing the NUMS OFF command from a command line.

8. Turn on insert mode; then insert spaces as necessary to align the labels and underscores to match Display 3.8.

When you are satisfied with the results, select **End** from the **File** menu, or issue the END command from a command line. The SAS System asks you the following question:

```
Have you added any computational or repeated fields (Y or N)? _
```

For this example, type N in the field provided because you have not created any special fields. This closes the FSEDIT Modify window and opens the FSEDIT Identify window.

In the FSEDIT Identify window, you tell the FSEDIT procedure where each variable field is located on the display. The procedure loses track of the location of a variable field when you modify any part of a line that contains that field. The FSEDIT Identify window prompts you to identify the location of each variable field that the procedure is unable to identify in the modified display. Follow the directions on the screen to identify the fields. When you finish, you see the following message at the top of the display:

```
NOTE:  All fields are identified.
```

Select **End** from the **View** menu, or issue the END command from a command line to close the FSEDIT Identify window and return to the FSEDIT Menu window. This saves the customized data entry display in the catalog entry that you specified in the PROC FSEDIT statement. Select **Goback** from the FSEDIT Menu window to return to the FSEDIT window, or select other menu options to further customize your application.

See Chapter 8, "Creating Data Entry Applications Using the FSEDIT Procedure," in *SAS/FSP Software: Usage and Reference* for more information.

Managing and Examining Survey Data

Data often come from separate sources and need to be combined into a single data set before you can analyze them. Also, you often need to examine the data for missing entries, incorrect entries, values out of range, and so on. SAS software provides many useful tools for these tasks.

Combining SAS Data Sets

The SAS System provides four basic methods for combining data sets:

concatenating
> combines two or more data sets one after the other into a single data set. You concatenate data sets using either the SET statement in a DATA step or the APPEND procedure.

interleaving
> combines individual sorted data sets into one sorted data set. The number of observations in the combined data set is always equal to the sum of the number of observations in each of the separate data sets. You interleave data sets using a SET statement accompanied by a BY statement.

merging
> combines observations from two or more data sets into a single observation in a new data set. A *one-to-one merge* combines observations based on their positions in the data set. A *match-merge* combines observations based on the values of one or more common variables. You merge data sets using the MERGE statement and, if you are performing a match-merge, a BY statement.

updating
> replaces the values of variables in one data set (the master data set) with nonmissing values from another data set (the transaction data set). You update a data set using the UPDATE statement accompanied by a BY statement.

Some SAS data sets are arranged or ordered such that combining them in the desired way is difficult. For some different approaches to combining SAS data sets, see Kretzman (1990) and Lessmann (1990).

Concatenating SAS Data Sets

Suppose you want to add information from five new respondents to the survey data in the SAS data set SURVEY1. Here are these five new observations, which are located in a separate SAS data set called ADD5:

```
IDNUM Q1 Q2 Q3
1005  1  1  16000
1011  0  0  10000
1024  1  0  9000
1032  1  1  17000
1039  0  1  10000
```

If you want these new observations added to the bottom of the SURVEY1 data set, you can simply concatenate them. The following SAS code shows how you can use a SET statement in a DATA step to concatenate the five new observations to SURVEY1:

```
data survey1;
   set survey1 add5;
run;
```

You can also use PROC APPEND to concatenate the new observations to the bottom of the SURVEY1 data set, as shown in the following SAS code:

```
proc append base=survey1 data=add5;
run;
```

For these data, both methods produce the same results. The following PROC PRINT step lists in Output 3.4 the SURVEY1 data set after the five new observations from the ADD5 data set have been concatenated to it:

```
proc print data=survey1;
   var idnum q1 q2 q3;
   title 'Five New Observations Concatenated to SURVEY1';
run;
```

Output 3.4
SURVEY1 Data Set
after Concatenation

```
                Five New Observations Concatenated to SURVEY1

          OBS    IDNUM    Q1     Q2         Q3

            1     1013    No     New    $20,000.00
            2     1014    No     Used   $12,000.00
            3     1019    No     Used   $10,000.00
            4     1022    Yes    Used    $7,000.00
            5     1027    No     New       $100.00
            6     1029    Yes    New    $18,000.00
            7     1033    No     Used         .
            8     1036    No     New    $18,000.00
            9     1037    Yes    New    $16,000.00
           10     1044    No     New    $12,000.00
           11     1046    No     Used    $8,000.00
           12     1050    Yes    Used   $10,000.00
           13     1005    Yes    New    $16,000.00
           14     1011    No     Used   $10,000.00
           15     1024    Yes    Used    $9,000.00
           16     1032    Yes    New    $17,000.00
           17     1039    No     New    $10,000.00
```

PROC APPEND concatenates much faster than the SET statement, particularly when the BASE= data set is large, because PROC APPEND doesn't process the observations from the BASE= data set. However, PROC APPEND can concatenate only two data sets, whereas the SET statement can concatenate any number of data sets. The two methods also differ depending on the attributes of the variables in the data sets to be concatenated. For more information on which method to choose for your applications, see Chapter 15, "Concatenating SAS Data Sets," in *SAS Language and Procedures: Usage.*

Interleaving SAS Data Sets

Suppose you want to add the five new observations of the ADD5 data set to the SURVEY1 data set, but you want the combined data set to be sorted according to the values of a variable in the data sets. Assume for this example that you have not previously concatenated any new data to your original SURVEY1 data set. You can interleave the two data sets using a SET statement and a BY statement in a DATA step.

Before you can interleave data sets, the data must be sorted by the same variable or variables you will use with the BY statement that accompanies your SET statement. Suppose you want the data sorted by the values in the Q3 variable (the amount of money each respondent would be willing to spend on their next car purchase). You can use the SORT procedure to sort the two data sets by Q3 before you interleave them. The following SAS code sorts the two data sets by Q3, interleaves them, and lists the combined data set in Output 3.5:

```
proc sort data=survey1;
   by q3;
run;

proc sort data=add5;
   by q3;
run;

data survey2;
   set survey1 add5;
   by q3;
run;

proc print data=survey2;
   var idnum q1 q2 q3;
   title 'Interleaving SURVEY1 and ADD5';
run;
```

Output 3.5
Results of
Interleaving Data
Sets

```
                    Interleaving SURVEY1 and ADD5

         OBS    IDNUM   Q1     Q2            Q3

          1     1033    No     Used          .
          2     1027    No     New        $100.00
          3     1022    Yes    Used      $7,000.00
          4     1046    No     Used      $8,000.00
          5     1024    Yes    Used      $9,000.00
          6     1019    No     Used     $10,000.00
          7     1050    Yes    Used     $10,000.00
          8     1011    No     Used     $10,000.00
          9     1039    No     New      $10,000.00
         10     1014    No     Used     $12,000.00
         11     1044    No     New      $12,000.00
         12     1037    Yes    New      $16,000.00
```

```
       13    1005    Yes    New    $16,000.00
       14    1032    Yes    New    $17,000.00
       15    1029    Yes    New    $18,000.00
       16    1036    No     New    $18,000.00
       17    1013    No     New    $20,000.00
```

The new data set SURVEY2 includes all observations from both data sets. Each BY group in the new data set contains observations from SURVEY1 followed by observations from ADD5. For example, there are four respondents for whom Q3=$10,000. The first two identification numbers are 1019 and 1050, which come from the original SURVEY1 data set. The last two identification numbers are 1011 and 1039, which come from the ADD5 data set.

Merging SAS Data Sets

To merge two or more data sets, you can perform either one-to-one merging or match-merging. In one-to-one merging, you don't use a BY statement. Observations are combined based on their positions in the input data sets. In match-merging, you use a BY statement to combine observations from the input data sets based on common BY groups. Match-merging is the only method of merging SAS data sets described in this chapter because it minimizes the possibility of errors and is more useful for most marketing data applications.

Suppose that you want to combine the survey data you collect from your respondents with information on your respondents' most recent car purchases and income levels. Recall from Chapter 2 that this information is contained in the SAS data set CARINFO. Both the SURVEY1 data set and the CARINFO data set contain a variable called IDNUM that identifies each individual. You can use the IDNUM variable as the BY variable for the merge.

Because you want to use IDNUM as the BY variable for the merge, you must sort SURVEY1 and CARINFO by IDNUM before merging the two data sets. The following PROC SORT steps sort the two data sets by the values of the IDNUM variable:

```
proc sort data=survey1;
   by idnum;
run;

proc sort data=carinfo;
   by idnum;
run;
```

The following SAS code merges SURVEY1 with CARINFO and prints the merged data set in Output 3.6. The IN= option in the MERGE statement tells the SAS System to create a new variable named S. When the the SURVEY1 data set contributes data to the current observation, the value of S is 1; otherwise, its value is 0. The subsetting IF statement causes the new data set to contain only those observations for which S = 1. Thus, the new merged data set NEWDATA contains only 12 observations corresponding to the 12 observations in the SURVEY1 data set.

```
data newdata;
   merge survey1 (in=S) carinfo;
   if S;
```

```
      by idnum;
run;

proc print data=newdata;
    title 'Merging SURVEY1 and CARINFO';
run;
```

Output 3.6
Results of Merging
SURVEY1 and
CARINFO

```
                        Merging SURVEY1 and CARINFO

    OBS  Q1   Q2         Q3   IDNUM    INCOME           YEARPUR  TYPE

     1   No   New   $20,000.00  1013   Over $60,000        1993   new
     2   No   Used  $12,000.00  1014   $20,001 - $40,000   1992   new
     3   No   Used  $10,000.00  1019   Over $60,000        1991   new
     4   Yes  Used   $7,000.00  1022   $40,001 - $60,000   1990   new
     5   No   New      $100.00  1027   $20,001 - $40,000   1989   new
     6   Yes  New   $18,000.00  1029   Over $60,000        1989   used
     7   No   Used         .    1033   Over $60,000        1992   used
     8   No   New   $18,000.00  1036   Over $60,000        1991   new
     9   Yes  New   $16,000.00  1037   $20,001 - $40,000   1990   used
    10   No   New   $12,000.00  1044   Over $60,000        1992   used
    11   No   Used   $8,000.00  1046   Over $60,000        1992   new
    12   Yes  Used  $10,000.00  1050   Over $60,000        1993   used
```

Updating SAS Data Sets

Suppose you want to replace the values of variables in one data set with new values from another data set. You update the original information in the *master data set* with new information in the *transaction data set*.

For example, suppose you have new information about five individuals in your CARINFO data set. This new information is contained in the SAS data set NEW5. CARINFO is the master data set, and NEW5 is the transaction data set. Five individuals have either moved into different income levels or purchased cars since the last time you updated the CARINFO data set. The following PROC PRINT step lists the five observations of the NEW5 data set in Output 3.7:

```
proc print data=new5;
    title 'NEW5 Data Set';
run;
```

Output 3.7
Five New
Observations in
NEW5 Data Set

```
                    NEW5 Data Set

    OBS   IDNUM      INCOME        YEARPUR  TYPE

     1    1003          .           1993   used
     2    1004   $40,001 - $60,000
     3    1010   Over $60,000
     4    1029          .           1993   new
     5    1042   $20,001 - $40,000  1993   new
```

Note that not all variables have nonmissing values in the NEW5 data set. Only the identifier variable (IDNUM) has nonmissing values for each observation. The other variables contain nonmissing values only when they contain changed information about the individual represented by each identification number.

The master data set and the transaction data set must be sorted by the same variable or variables you specify in the BY statement accompanying the UPDATE statement. In this example, you use IDNUM as the BY variable in the following PROC SORT steps:

```
proc sort data=carinfo;
   by idnum;
run;

proc sort data=new5;
   by idnum;
run;
```

The following SAS code shows how to use the UPDATE statement to update CARINFO with the new information in NEW5:

```
data info2;
   update carinfo new5;
   by idnum;
run;
```

The following PROC PRINT step lists the first five observations of the master data set CARINFO, followed by the first five observations of the updated data set INFO2 in Output 3.8, showing how the master data set is updated by the transaction data set:

```
proc print data=carinfo(obs=5);
   title 'First Five Observations of the CARINFO Data Set';
   title2 'Original Master Data Set';
run;

proc print data=info2(obs=5);
   title 'First Five Observations of the INFO2 Data Set';
   title2 'Updated Master Data Set';
run;
```

Output 3.8
Partial Listing of Master Data Set and Updated Data Set

```
          First Five Observations of the CARINFO Data Set          1
                    Original Master Data Set

    OBS       INCOME          IDNUM   YEARPUR   TYPE

     1    $20,001 - $40,000    1001     1987    used
     2    Under $20,000        1002     1986    used
     3    $40,001 - $60,000    1003     1988    used
     4    Over $60,000         1004     1989    new
     5    Over $60,000         1005     1992    new
```

```
                    Updated Master Data Set

         OBS       INCOME          IDNUM   YEARPUR   TYPE

          1    $20,001 - $40,000   1001     1987     used
          2    Under $20,000       1002     1986     used
          3    $40,001 - $60,000   1003     1993     used
          4    $40,001 - $60,000   1004     1989     new
          5    Over $60,000        1005     1992     new
```

In Output 3.8, you can see that the individual represented by identification number 1003 purchased a used car in 1993, and the individual represented by identification number 1004 changed to a lower income level.

Examining Data

You often need to examine your data to check for missing values, duplicate values, values out of range, invalid data, and so on. You can use the SAS System to help perform these tasks. In addition to the SORT and UNIVARIATE procedures described in the following sections, you can also use the CHART, CORR, FREQ, MEANS, SUMMARY, and TABULATE procedures to examine your data. See the *SAS Procedures Guide* for more information on these procedures.

Deleting Duplicate Observations

Suppose your SURVEY1 data set contains a duplicate observation for IDNUM=1022. This could occur due to an error in data entry or an error in manipulating the SURVEY1 data set. The data are shown here:

```
IDNUM Q1 Q2 Q3
1013  0  1  20000
1014  0  0  12000
1019  0  0  10000
1022  1  0  7000
1022  1  0  7000
1027  0  1  100
1029  1  1  18000
1033  0  0  .
1036  0  1  18000
1037  1  1  16000
1044  0  1  12000
1046  0  0  8000
1050  1  0  10000
```

You can use the SORT procedure to remove duplicate observations from your SAS data sets. The NODUPLICATES option in the PROC SORT statement deletes any observation that duplicates the values of all variables (both BY variables and other variables) of another observation in the data set. The following steps sort SURVEY1, remove the duplicate

observation, and create a new data set called SURVEY1X. Output 3.9 shows the message
that appears in the SAS log and the data set that results.

```
proc sort data=survey1 out=survey1x noduplicates;
   by idnum;
run;

proc print data=survey1x;
   var idnum q1 q2 q3;
   title 'SURVEY1X Data Set';
   title2 'Sorting with the NODUPLICATES Option'
run;
```

Output 3.9
Removing a
Duplicate
Observation with
PROC SORT

```
3  proc sort data=survey1 out=survey1x noduplicates;
4     by idnum;
5  run;

NOTE: 1 duplicate observations were deleted.
NOTE: The data set WORK.SURVEY1X has 12 observations and 4 variables.
NOTE: The PROCEDURE SORT used 0:00:01.0 real 0:00:00.0 cpu.

6
7  proc print data=survey1x;
8     var idnum q1 q2 q3;
9     title 'SURVEY1X Data Set';
10    title2 'Sorting with the NODUPLICATES Option';
11 run;

NOTE: The PROCEDURE PRINT used 0:00:00.0 real 0:00:00.0 cpu.
```

```
                         SURVEY1X Data Set                    1
                   Sorting with the NODUPLICATES Option

         OBS    IDNUM    Q1     Q2           Q3

          1     1013     No     New      $20,000.00
          2     1014     No     Used     $12,000.00
          3     1019     No     Used     $10,000.00
          4     1022     Yes    Used      $7,000.00
          5     1027     No     New         $100.00
          6     1029     Yes    New      $18,000.00
          7     1033     No     Used          .
          8     1036     No     New      $18,000.00
          9     1037     Yes    New      $16,000.00
         10     1044     No     New      $12,000.00
         11     1046     No     Used      $8,000.00
         12     1050     Yes    Used     $10,000.00
```

Using the UNIVARIATE Procedure to Examine Quantitative Data

Use the UNIVARIATE procedure to determine if your quantitative data have appropriate
central tendency (mean, median) and variability (variance, standard deviation). PROC
UNIVARIATE also identifies extreme values in your variables. For a more complete
description of PROC UNIVARIATE and more examples showing how it can be useful, see
Chapter 6, "Analyzing Quantitative Marketing Data."

The following SAS program uses PROC UNIVARIATE to examine the data in the SURVEY1 data set created earlier in this chapter:

```
proc univariate data=survey1;
   var q1 q2 q3;
   title 'Examining Survey Data';
run;
```

The previous SAS statements produce three pages of output for each variable listed in the VAR statement. Only the output for the Q3 variable is shown in Output 3.10.

Output 3.10
Partial Listing of
PROC
UNIVARIATE
Output

```
                           Examining Survey Data                          1

                            Univariate Procedure

        Variable=Q3

                                 Moments

                  N              11   Sum Wgts          11
                  Mean     11918.18   Sum           131100
                  Std Dev  5852.661   Variance    34253636
                  Skewness -0.48656   Kurtosis    0.151452
                  USS       1.905E9   CSS          3.4254E8
                  CV       49.10699   Std Mean    1764.644
                  T:Mean=0 6.753875   Pr>|T|        0.0001
                  Num ^= 0       11   Num > 0           11
                  M(Sign)       5.5   Pr>=|M|       0.0010
                  Sgn Rank       33   Pr>=|S|       0.0010
```

```
                           Examining Survey Data                          2

                            Univariate Procedure

        Variable=Q3

                             Quantiles(Def=5)

               100% Max    20000       99%    20000
                75% Q3     18000       95%    20000
                50% Med    12000       90%    18000
                25% Q1      8000       10%     7000
                 0% Min      100        5%      100
                                        1%      100
               Range       19900
               Q3-Q1       10000
               Mode        10000
```

```
                           Examining Survey Data                          3

                            Univariate Procedure

        Variable=Q3

                                Extremes

                Lowest   Obs      Highest   Obs
                  100(     5)      12000(    10)
                 7000(     4)      16000(     9)
                 8000(    11)      18000(     6)
```

```
                          10000(    12)    18000(     8)
                          10000(     3)    20000(     1)


                          Missing Value          .
                          Count                  1
                          % Count/Nobs        8.33
```

Interpretation of output

The first page of PROC UNIVARIATE output lists the moments for the Q3 variable, such as the mean and standard deviation. The second page lists quantiles, including the median, and also lists the minimum and maximum values. The third page identifies the five lowest and five highest values. Note that Q3 has a minimum value of **$100**, which might be a correct entry, a mistake in data entry, or a mistake on the part of the respondent. You should examine that observation carefully to determine if you need to delete it or get more information from the respondent, if possible. PROC UNIVARIATE also notes how many observations have missing values and what percentage of the total observations are missing.

Learning More

□ For complete reference and usage information on the FSEDIT and FSVIEW procedures and SAS/FSP, see *SAS/FSP Software: Usage and Reference, Version 6, First Edition.*

□ For more information on data entry, combining data sets, manipulating data, and examining data for errors, see *SAS Language and Procedures: Usage, Version 6, First Edition* and *SAS Language and Procedures: Usage 2, Version 6, First Edition.*

□ For a comparison of procedures useful for calculating descriptive statistics for survey data, see Chapter 1, "SAS Elementary Statistics Procedures," in the *SAS Procedures Guide, Version 6, Third Edition.*

□ For more information on the BY, FILENAME, FORMAT, MERGE, PUT, SET, and UPDATE statements and the DATA step, see *SAS Language: Reference, Version 6, First Edition.*

□ For complete reference information on the APPEND, FORMAT, FORMS, SORT and UNIVARIATE procedures, see the *SAS Procedures Guide.*

References

□ Kretzman, P. (1990), "Mortar and Bricks: Using Basic SAS System Procedures to Manipulate Your Data," *Proceedings of the Fifteenth Annual SAS Users Group International*, 155-162.

□ Lessmann, T. (1990), "A Solution to Unique Match-Merge Situations," *Proceedings of the Fifteenth Annual SAS Users Group International*, 910-915.

Chapter **4** Producing Marketing Reports

Introduction

This chapter presents examples showing how to use the SAS System to produce various types of marketing reports, including the following:

- tabular reports

- plots of data over time

- block charts, bar charts, and pie charts

- block maps and choropleth maps.

The SAS System provides a wide range of reporting capabilities. Only a portion of these capabilities is presented in this chapter. For more information, see *Report Writing with SAS Software: Examples.*

This chapter shows how you can use the following components of the SAS System to produce marketing reports:

base SAS software
> includes the PLOT, PRINT, REPORT, and TABULATE procedures. Each of these procedures offers a different set of features and advantages, providing a wide range of reporting capabilities.

SAS/ASSIST software
> provides a task-oriented, point-and-click interface to the entire SAS System. You can produce most of the different types of reports or graphics available in the SAS System by using SAS/ASSIST.

SAS/GRAPH software
> includes the GCHART, GMAP, and GPLOT procedures. These procedures give you the ability to produce high-resolution graphics charts, maps, and plots, in color or in black-and-white.

Producing Tabular Reports

You can use the examples in this section to produce tabular reports for data stored in a SAS data set. Although the examples in this section use prospective sales data, you can use the same methods to produce virtually any type of report. The examples show how to use the following base SAS procedures:

□ the PRINT procedure

□ the REPORT procedure

□ the TABULATE procedure.

The procedure you choose depends on what type of control you want over the layout of the report. PROC PRINT gives you the least control, but it provides quick and simple reports where presentation quality is not of utmost importance. PROC REPORT offers moderate control over the layout of the report. You have the choice of using an interactive windowing environment or a noninteractive mode for writing reports with PROC REPORT. PROC TABULATE produces well-polished tabular reports.

You can also use a DATA step to write reports. A DATA step offers maximum control and flexibility, but at the expense of more time and effort than if you use one of the prebuilt report-writing procedures. See Chapter 29, "Writing Output," and Chapter 30, "Customizing Output," in *SAS Language and Procedures: Usage* for more information.

Example Data for Tabular Reports

Suppose you have information on one car manufacturer's prospective new car sales for each state and the District of Columbia in the United States. Each state is assigned to one of four geographic sales regions: Midwest, Northeast, South, or West. The prospective sales data come from sales forecasts based on analysis of historical car sales data from each state. For more information on forecasting sales data, see the *SAS/ETS User's Guide* or *SAS/ETS Software: Applications Guide 1.* These (hypothetical) prospective sales data are stored in a SAS data set called CARSALES. The full data set (153 observations) and the DATA step used to create it are listed in the appendix. The following list describes the variables in the CARSALES data set:

REGION   is one of four geographic sales regions.

STATENM   is the two-character postal code abbreviation for each state.

STYLE   is the style of the car — sedan, coupe, or wagon.

QUANTITY   is the forecast number of cars sold.

REVENUE   is the forecast dollar value of car sales (in $1,000).

A partial listing of the data appears as follows:

```
REGION      STATENM    STYLE     QUANTITY    REVENUE

Midwest     IA         coupe       200        3671
Midwest     IA         sedan       252        3863
Midwest     IA         wagon       263        4362
Midwest     IL         coupe       374        6964
Midwest     IL         sedan       485        7493
Midwest     IL         wagon       188        3111
Midwest     IN         coupe       330        6111
Midwest     IN         sedan       123        1890
Midwest     IN         wagon       108        1748
```

Producing Quick Reports with the PRINT Procedure

To produce a quick report listing the quantity and dollar amounts of prospective sales, you can use the PROC PRINT step. The example in this section shows how to produce a prospective sales report for a portion of the CARSALES data set.

Because the data set in this example is large, producing separate reports for subsets of the full data set is more informative than trying to produce a report for the full data set. You can use WHERE processing to list only a portion of a larger data set. In this example, you use a WHERE statement to select only those observations from the CARSALES data set that are assigned to the Midwest sales region.

You can change the expression in the WHERE statement to select other subsets of observations from the data set. The subset you select depends on your purpose in producing the report. For example, if you want to compare sales for a specific style of car across geographic regions, you would select only those observations for that specific style of car (for example, sedan).

The first step in producing the prospective sales report in this example is to use the SORT procedure to sort the data set by style of car and by descending levels of sales quantity. Use the statements and options described in the following list to perform the sorting:

PROC SORT statement
    invokes the procedure and enables you to specify the input and output data sets.

DATA= option   names the SAS data set that you want to sort.

OUT= option   specifies a name for the sorted output data set. The DROP= data set option excludes the specified variables from the output data set. In this example, you exclude REGION from the output data set because all observations in the output data set have the same value of REGION.

WHERE statement
selects observations from a SAS data set that meet a particular condition. In this example, you select only those observations that are in the Midwest sales region.

BY statement
specifies the variables by which the data set is sorted. The DESCENDING option sorts the data by the descending values of the variable specified after this option. In this example, you sort the data set first by ascending order of STYLE values, then by descending order of QUANTITY values:

```
proc sort data=carsales out=cars1(drop=region);
   where region='Midwest';
   by style descending quantity;
run;
```

The previous statements produce an output data set called CARS1. Use this data set as input to PROC PRINT to produce the prospective sales report for the Midwest sales region.

The example in this section produces a report with separate subtotals for each level of the specified sorting variable. In this example, STYLE is the sorting variable. Use a BY statement in the PROC PRINT step to obtain separate analyses for each style of car. PROC PRINT expects the data to be sorted by the values of the BY variable. The previous PROC SORT step sorts the data set appropriately.

The following list describes some of the statements and options used in the example program:

□ The LABEL option uses variables' labels as column headings. The variable labels for the CARSALES data set are specified in the DATA step, as shown in the appendix.

□ The ID statement used with a BY statement prints the BY variable beside each BY grouping. If you omit the ID statement, the BY variable is printed above each BY grouping.

□ The SUM statement produces subtotals for QUANTITY and REVENUE for each style of car and totals for QUANTITY and REVENUE at the bottom of the output.

□ The VAR statement requests that PROC PRINT list the specified variables. PROC PRINT also lists all variables specified on the SUM statement even if they are omitted from the VAR statement.

The following statements produce the tabular prospective sales report shown in Output 4.1:

```
proc print data=cars1 label;
   by style;
   id style;
   sum quantity revenue;
   var statenm quantity revenue;
   title3 'Midwest Region';
run;
```

Output 4.1
Using PROC PRINT
to Produce a Report

```
                        Car Sales Data
                    Prospective Sales Figures
                        Midwest Region

                                     Sales
                              Sales  Revenue
         Style   State     Quantity  (in $1000)

         coupe    IL         374      $6,964
                  MO         366      $6,588
                  IN         330      $6,111
                  OH         238      $4,321
                  IA         200      $3,671
                  MN         200      $3,670
                  WI         166      $3,004
                  MI         163      $3,003
         -----              --------  ----------
         coupe             2037      $37,332

         sedan    MO         506      $7,806
                  MI         486      $7,508
                  IL         485      $7,493
                  OH         408      $6,164
                  WI         312      $4,755
                  MN         253      $3,865
                  IA         252      $3,863
                  IN         123      $1,890
         -----              --------  ----------
         sedan             2825      $43,344

         wagon    OH         275      $4,491
                  IA         263      $4,362
                  WI         259      $4,211
                  IL         188      $3,111
                  MO         180      $2,907
                  MN         174      $2,862
                  MI         167      $2,749
                  IN         108      $1,748
         -----              --------  ----------
         wagon             1614      $26,441
                           ========  ==========
                           6476     $107,117
```

Customizing Reports with the REPORT Procedure

Use the REPORT procedure when you want more control over the appearance of your report than that offered by PROC PRINT. PROC REPORT combines features from the PRINT, MEANS, and TABULATE procedures with features of DATA-step report writing into a powerful report-writing tool. PROC REPORT offers an interactive windowing environment for producing reports. You may also invoke PROC REPORT in a nonwindowing environment, in which case you submit a series of statements with the PROC REPORT statement, just as you do in other SAS procedures.

Instead of producing a report for the full CARSALES data set, in this example you produce an informative report based on a summary of the data. Use the SORT procedure to sort the data and the MEANS procedure to summarize the data before producing the report with PROC REPORT. The statements and options described in the following list create an output data set that contains a summary of the car sales data:

PROC MEANS statement
> invokes the procedure and enables you to specify an input data set with the DATA= option. The NOPRINT option suppresses printing of output.

VAR statement
> specifies variables for which statistics are to be calculated.

BY statement
> produces separate analyses for the specified variables. PROC MEANS expects the input data set to be sorted according to the values of the BY variables.

OUTPUT statement
> requests that PROC MEANS write statistics to a new data set. Specify the following options for the output data set:

OUT= option	names the output data set.
DROP= data set option	excludes the _TYPE_ and _FREQ_ variables from the output data set. PROC MEANS creates these two variables when you write statistics to an output data set.
SUM= option	specifies that the sums of the variables specified in the VAR statement be calculated and written to the output data set. The expression SUM=; causes PROC MEANS to use the same name for the sum statistics in the output data set as the name of the corresponding variable in the input data set.

First, use PROC SORT to sort the CARSALES data by the values of REGION and STYLE so that the data are in the proper order for the BY statement in the PROC MEANS step. PROC SORT creates an output data set called CARS2, which you use as the input data set for PROC MEANS, as shown in the following statements:

```
proc sort data=carsales out=cars2;
   by region style;
run;

proc means data=cars2 noprint;
   var quantity revenue;
   by region style;
   output out=cars3(drop=_type_ _freq_) sum=;
run;
```

The previous statements create the CARS3 data set, which contains a summary of the CARSALES data set. The example in this section uses the CARS3 data set to produce a customized summary report. To invoke the REPORT procedure in a windowing environment, submit the following statements, which create the basic report shown in the REPORT window in Display 4.1:

```
proc report data=cars3;
   title3 'Summary Report';
run;
```

Display 4.1
PROC REPORT
Window for
Summarized Car
Sales Data

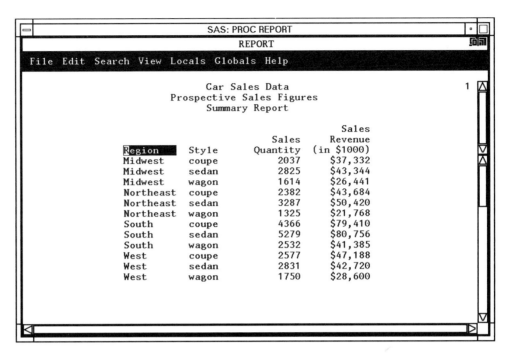

With PROC REPORT, you can perform tasks such as the following to enhance your reports:

□ change the spacing between rows

□ create groups of observations

□ create subtotals and summaries for numeric variables

□ add break lines.

Display 4.2 shows an example of the basic report revised with the windowing environment of PROC REPORT. Only the upper portion of the report is shown in Display 4.2 because the full report does not fit inside one window.

Display 4.2
Revised Report for
Summarized Car
Sales Data

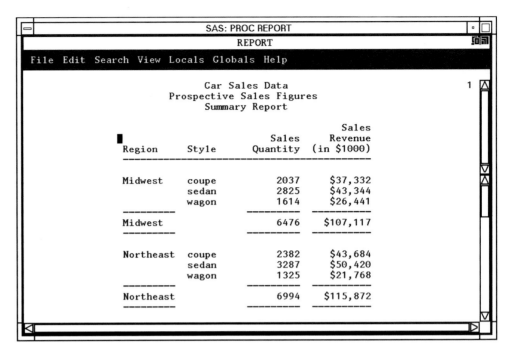

To customize the basic report shown in Display 4.1 so that it looks like the report shown in Display 4.2, follow these steps:

1. Select **ROptions** from the **Locals** menu to open the ROPTIONS window. Select **HEADLINE** and **HEADSKIP** from this window; then select **OK** to return to the REPORT window. This adds a line and a line space after the column headings.

2. Select **RBreak** from the **Edit** menu to open the LOCATION window. Select **After detail** and then select **OK** in the LOCATION window to open the BREAK window. Select **DOUBLE OVERLINE (=)**, **DOUBLE UNDERLINE (=)**, **SKIP**, and **SUMMARIZE** from the BREAK window. This creates break lines at the bottom of the table and computes a total for the two analysis variables (QUANTITY and REVENUE).

3. Still in the BREAK window, select **Edit Program** to open the COMPUTE window. Type in **region='Total:';**, then select **End** from the **File** menu to run the program, exit the COMPUTE window, and return to the BREAK window. Select **OK** to return to the REPORT window. This prints **Total:** at the bottom of the REGION column.

4. Select the REGION variable column. Then, select **Define** from the **Edit** menu to open the DEFINITION window. Select **GROUP** from the DEFINITION window to define REGION as a grouping variable. Select **OK** to return to the REPORT window.

5. With the REGION variable column still selected, select **Break** from the **Edit** menu. Select **After detail** and then **OK** from the LOCATION window to open the BREAK window. Select **OVERLINE**, **UNDERLINE**, **SKIP**, and **SUMMARIZE** from the Break window. This creates subtotals for each value of region and sets off the subtotals with break lines. Select **OK** to return to the REPORT window.

Only the first page of the customized report is shown in Display 4.2. Use scroll bars or the scrolling commands from the **View** menu to see the rest of the report. For more details on creating customized reports with PROC REPORT, see the *SAS Guide to the REPORT Procedure.*

You can save a report definition in a file so that you do not need to redefine it each time you want to display or print the report. Select **RStore** from the **File** menu to save a report definition in a file. Select **RLoad** from the **File** menu to load a report definition into the REPORT window. For this example, the definition of the report shown in Display 4.2 is stored in a file called CARSALES within a SAS catalog called MASTER.REPORTS. The name MASTER is a libref that you have assigned to a permanent SAS data library. All report definitions are stored as entries of type REPT in the SAS catalog. To display the full report in the OUTPUT window, issue the following statements. The REPORT= option identifies the location of the stored report. The NOWD option causes PROC REPORT to display the report in the OUTPUT window rather than in the REPORT window. The report is shown in Output 4.2.

```
proc report report=master.reports.carsales nowd;
run;
```

Output 4.2
Full Summary
Report for
Prospective Car
Sales Data

```
                              Car Sales Data
                          Prospective Sales Figures
                              Summary Report

                                              Sales
                                     Sales     Revenue
             Region    Style      Quantity   (in $1000)
             --------------------------------------------

             Midwest   coupe          2037      $37,332
                       sedan          2825      $43,344
                       wagon          1614      $26,441
             ---------            ---------    ---------
             Midwest                  6476     $107,117
             ---------            ---------    ---------


             Northeast coupe          2382      $43,684
                       sedan          3287      $50,420
                       wagon          1325      $21,768
             ---------            ---------    ---------
             Northeast                6994     $115,872
             ---------            ---------    ---------


             South     coupe          4366      $79,410
                       sedan          5279      $80,756
                       wagon          2532      $41,385
             ---------            ---------    ---------
             South                   12177     $201,551
             ---------            ---------    ---------


             West      coupe          2577      $47,188
                       sedan          2831      $42,720
                       wagon          1750      $28,600
             ---------            ---------    ---------
             West                     7158     $118,508
             ---------            ---------    ---------


             =========            =========   ==========
             Total:                  32805     $543,048
             =========            =========   ==========
```

Using the REPORT Language

You can use PROC REPORT to produce a sales report in a batch environment by submitting SAS statements, just as you do for other procedures.

The following SAS statements and options produce the revised sales report shown previously in Display 4.2 and Output 4.2. For information on the statements and options used in this sample program, see the *SAS Guide to the REPORT Procedure*, or SAS Technical Report P-258, *Using the REPORT Procedure in a Nonwindowing Environment*,

Release 6.07. If you invoke PROC REPORT in a windowing environment, you can still produce a listing of SAS code that you can use to create the same report in a batch environment. To view the SAS code, select `List` from the `Locals` menu. Then you can print the code or save it to a file.

```
proc report ls=76  ps=60  split="/" headline headskip center;
   column region style quantity revenue;
   define region / group format=$9. width=9 spacing=2 left "Region";
   define style / display format=$8. width=8 spacing=2 left "Style";
   define quantity / sum format=best9. width=9 spacing=2 right
                  "Sales Quantity";
   define revenue / sum format=dollar10. width=10 spacing=2 right
                  "Sales Revenue (in $1000)";
   break after region / ol ul skip summarize;
   rbreak after / dol dul skip summarize;
   compute after;
      region='Total:';
   endcomp;
run;
```

Producing Stub-and-Banner Tables with the TABULATE Procedure

Stub-and-banner tables are a way to present two-way tables of data. The rows, or stubs, of the table correspond to the levels of one or more nested variables, and the columns, or banner, also correspond to the nested levels of one or more variables. In some cases, stub-and-banner tables can be as simple as a two-variable crosstabulation table. In other cases, however, stub-and-banner tables can have multiple variables in the stubs or banner and can contain various statistics and significance tests for the values in the table.

The TABULATE procedure produces stub-and-banner tables for SAS data sets. You use the TABLE statement in PROC TABULATE to specify most of the details about the table. The next section describes the TABLE statement in more detail. For complete information on PROC TABULATE, see the *SAS Guide to TABULATE Processing*.

Describing the TABLE Statement in the TABULATE Procedure

A TABLE statement consists of one to three *dimension expressions* separated by commas that can be followed by an option list. If all three dimensions are specified, the leftmost dimension defines pages, the middle defines rows, and the rightmost defines columns. If two dimensions are specified, the left defines rows, and the right defines columns. If a single dimension is specified, it defines columns.

Row expressions and column expressions are defined the same way and are referred to collectively as dimension expressions. A dimension expression is composed of elements and operators.

The elements you can use in a dimension expression are

□ analysis variables that you specify in a VAR statement.

□ class variables that you specify in a CLASS statement.

□ the universal class variable ALL, which summarizes all of the categories for class variables in the same parenthetical group or dimension (if the variable ALL is not contained in a parenthetical group).

□   keywords for statistics.

□   format modifiers, which define how to format values in cells of the table. These have the form *f=format* and must be crossed with the elements that produce the cells you want to format.

□   labels, which temporarily replace the names of variables and statistics with a label. These have the form ='*label*' and affect only the variable or statistic that immediately precedes the label.

A dimension expression can have any of the following forms:

element*element (crossing)
>   creates categories from the combination of values of the variables. If one of the elements in the crossing is an analysis variable, the statistics for the analysis variable are calculated for the categories created by the class variables.

element element (concatenation)
>   joins information for the elements by placing the output for the second element immediately after the output for the first element.

(*element element*) (grouping)
>   causes the operator adjacent to the parenthesis to be applied to each concatenated element inside the parentheses.

Table 4.1 lists the operators and the effects they produce:

Table 4.1
Effects of Operators in the TABLE Statement of PROC TABULATE

Operator	Description	Action
,	(comma)	separates dimensions of a table and crosses elements across dimensions
*	(asterisk)	crosses elements within a dimension
	(blank space)	concatenates elements in a dimension
()	(parentheses)	group elements and associate an operator with an entire group
<>	(brackets)	specify *denominator definitions* for percentages
=	(equal sign)	assigns a label to a variable or statistic, or completes a format modifier

You specify denominator definitions when you want to show percentages in the table. Because percentages can be calculated in different ways, you must specify the denominator of the percentage calculation. For example, you can express cell frequencies as a percentage of the entire table, of a column, or of a row.

TABULATE Procedure Example

The statements and options of the PROC TABULATE step described in the following list produce a stub-and-banner table for the prospective car sales data:

OPTIONS statement
> specifies a larger line size with the LINESIZE= option to accommodate the table.

PROC TABULATE statement
> invokes the procedure and enables you to specify options:

> DATA= option   names the input SAS data set. In this example, you use the full CARSALES data set as input.

> FORMAT= option   specifies a default format for all cells in the table. This format is overridden by any formats specified in a TABLE statement.

CLASS statement
> identifies variables in the input data set as class variables. Normally, each class variable has a small number of discrete values or unique levels.

TABLE statement
> describes the table to be printed. A TABLE statement is required for every PROC TABULATE step. See "Describing the TABLE Statement in the TABULATE Procedure" for more information. In this example, you request the calculation of the SUM statistic for the two numeric variables, QUANTITY and REVENUE.

> RTS= option   specifies the number of print positions allotted to the headings in the row dimension. The default value is one-fourth of the LINESIZE= value.

Note: Sometimes, each observation in the input data set represents *n* observations, rather than a single observation. In such cases, you should use the FREQ statement to specify the variable in the input data set whose values represent the frequency of the observation.

The stub-and-banner table produced by the following SAS program is shown in Output 4.3:

```
options linesize=105;
proc tabulate data=carsales format=8.;
   class region style;
   var quantity revenue;
   table region='Sales Region' all='All Regions',
         (style='Style' all='All Styles')*
         (quantity='Sales Quantity'
         revenue='Sales Revenue (in $1000)'*f=dollar10.0)*sum=' ' /
         rts=16;
run;
```

Output 4.3 *Stub-and-Banner Table Produced by PROC TABULATE*

```
                                 Car Sales Data
                              Prospective Sales Figures

     -------------------------------------------------------------------------------
     |             |                          Style                   |            |
     |             |-------------------------------------------------|            |
     |             |    coupe     |    sedan     |    wagon     | All Styles |
     |             |--------------+--------------+--------------+------------|
     |             |      | Sales |      | Sales |      | Sales |      | Sales |
     |             | Sales| Revenue| Sales| Revenue| Sales| Revenue| Sales| Revenue|
     |             |Quantity|(in $1000)|Quantity|(in $1000)|Quantity|(in $1000)|Quantity|(in $1000)|
     |-------------+--------+----------+--------+----------+--------+----------+--------+----------|
     |Sales Region |        |          |        |          |        |          |        |          |
     |-------------|        |          |        |          |        |          |        |          |
     |Midwest      |   2037 |  $37,332 |   2825 |  $43,344 |   1614 |  $26,441 |   6476 | $107,117 |
     |-------------+--------+----------+--------+----------+--------+----------+--------+----------|
     |Northeast    |   2382 |  $43,684 |   3287 |  $50,420 |   1325 |  $21,768 |   6994 | $115,872 |
     |-------------+--------+----------+--------+----------+--------+----------+--------+----------|
     |South        |   4366 |  $79,410 |   5279 |  $80,756 |   2532 |  $41,385 |  12177 | $201,551 |
     |-------------+--------+----------+--------+----------+--------+----------+--------+----------|
     |West         |   2577 |  $47,188 |   2831 |  $42,720 |   1750 |  $28,600 |   7158 | $118,508 |
     |-------------+--------+----------+--------+----------+--------+----------+--------+----------|
     |All Regions  |  11362 | $207,614 |  14222 | $217,240 |   7221 | $118,194 |  32805 | $543,048 |
     -------------------------------------------------------------------------------
```

Using SAS/ASSIST Software to Produce Reports

SAS/ASSIST software is a menu-driven, task-oriented interface to the SAS System. You can use SAS/ASSIST software to access the power of the SAS System quickly and easily without having to learn SAS programming statements. To choose a task within SAS/ASSIST software, you tab to it and press ENTER. Or, if you have a mouse, you can point to the task and click with the mouse.

Additionally, SAS/ASSIST software builds and documents an English-like SAS program for each task you perform. You can view and modify these SAS programs and their output. Experienced users can use these programs as a basis for customized applications.

You can invoke SAS/ASSIST software in one of three ways:

□ Select **SAS/ASSIST** from the **Globals** menu in the SAS Display Manager system.

□ Type ASSIST on the command line.

□ Use a function key predefined to invoke SAS/ASSIST.

When you invoke SAS/ASSIST software, you see the SAS/ASSIST primary menu, as shown in Display 4.3.

Display 4.3
SAS/ASSIST
Primary Menu

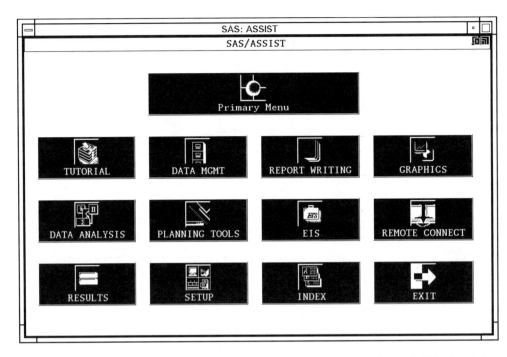

Select **REPORT WRITING** to bring up the report writing menu, as shown in Display 4.4.

Display 4.4
SAS/ASSIST Report
Writing Menu

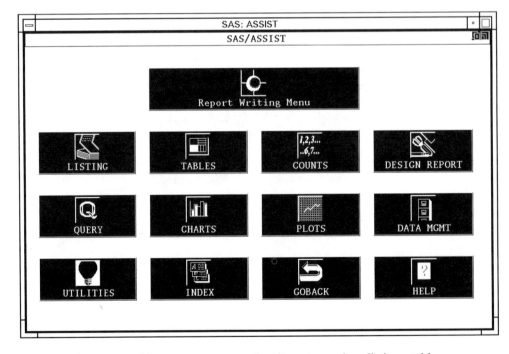

From the report writing menu, you can select items to produce listings, tables, crosstabulations, charts, plots, and various other types of reports. For example, if you select the **TABLES** item from the report writing menu, you make selections from other menus that become increasingly specific. That is, you select

□ one of six different table styles from templates displayed on the screen

□ the variables you want to appear in the selected table style

□ the statistics you want computed for the selected variables

□ additional options, such as formats, data order, spacing, labels, and handling of missing data.

You can also select **GRAPHICS** from the SAS/ASSIST primary menu to produce either high-resolution or low-resolution graphics charts, plots, and maps. SAS/ASSIST can help you produce any of the reports and graphics shown in this chapter.

Graphing Marketing Data

A visual representation of data often provides useful information that may not be readily apparent in lists or summaries. You can use the PLOT procedure in base SAS software, or the GPLOT or GCHART procedures in SAS/GRAPH software for plots and charts of marketing data. You can use the GMAP procedure in SAS/GRAPH software to produce maps of geographic marketing data. The following sections show examples of how to use these procedures.

You need to specify a device driver to run SAS/GRAPH software. You can do this in the GOPTIONS statement by specifying the DEVICE= option using the following form: DEVICE=*device-driver-name.*

See *SAS/GRAPH Software: Reference* for more information on setting graphics options, specifying device drivers, and other details of SAS/GRAPH software.

Producing Plots

Plots are useful for examining trends and shapes in data. They are particularly useful for plotting data against time. The PLOT procedure in base SAS software produces line-printer-quality plots, and the GPLOT procedure in SAS/GRAPH software produces high-resolution plots. Examples in the following sections show how to use these two procedures to produce plots of data.

Suppose you want to produce a report on the actual sales trends for each of three different styles of cars during 1993. First, you must work with the data to get it in the proper form for plotting.

Getting the Data into Shape for Plotting

Suppose you have a file of information on car purchases during 1993. In this file, you have the date and style of car purchased. If you have one record for each car that was purchased during 1993, you will have a very large amount of data, and it can be difficult to produce a meaningful plot of these data in their original form. You can make better use of the data by crosstabulating them and plotting the crosstabulations. This section shows how you can

□ enter the car sales data into a SAS data set.

□ produce crosstabulations of the car sales data using the FREQ procedure.

□ print the crosstabulated car sales data.

The following DATA step shows how you can enter the (hypothetical) car sales information into a SAS data set called CARTIME. The PDATE variable is the date that the car was purchased. Enter this variable into the CARTIME data set with a MMDDYY. informat. Then use the FORMAT statement to assign the MONYY. format to the PDATE variable so that it appears with the MONYY. format in output. For this example, using the MONYY. format reduces the number of different levels of the PDATE variable to 12 — one for each month.

```
data cartime;
    informat pdate mmddyy.;
    format pdate monyy.;
    label pdate='Purchase Date'
          style='Car Style'
    input pdate style $;
    cards;
010493 coupe
010493 sedan
010593 sedan
010593 wagon
010693 sedan
010793 coupe
010793 sedan
  .
  .
  .
more data lines
  .
  .
  .
;
```

Use the following statements and options in the FREQ procedure to crosstabulate the car sales data:

PROC FREQ statement
> invokes the procedure and enables you to specify the input data set with the DATA= option.

TABLES statement
> specifies the crosstabulation of variables in the input data set. In this example, the STYLE variable is crosstabulated with the PDATE variable.

> NOPRINT option   suppresses printing of crosstabulation tables.

> OUT= option   creates an output SAS data set containing variable values and frequency counts.

In this example, the OUT= data set CAROUT contains one observation for each combination of STYLE and PDATE. The output data set also contains the variables COUNT and PERCENT. COUNT's value in each observation is the number of observations in the original data set, CARTIME, that have the given combination of STYLE and PDATE values; PERCENT's value is the percent of the total number of observations having that combination of STYLE and PDATE.

```
proc freq data=cartime;
    tables pdate*style / noprint out=carout;
run;
```

The following PROC PRINT step lists the CAROUT data in Output 4.4. The LABEL option in the PROC PRINT statement uses variables' labels as column headings.

```
/* Title statement used for data listing and plots */
title 'New Car Sales for 1993';

proc print data=carout label;
run;
```

Output 4.4
Listing of Output
Data Set from
PROC FREQ

```
                          New Car Sales for 1993

                                                    Percent of
                  Purchase    Car     Frequency       Total
          OBS      Date      Style      Count       Frequency

           1      JAN93     coupe        495         2.7578
           2      JAN93     sedan        750         4.1785
           3      JAN93     wagon        375         2.0893
           4      FEB93     coupe        304         1.6937
           5      FEB93     sedan        665         3.7049
           6      FEB93     wagon        298         1.6603
           7      MAR93     coupe        507         2.8247
           8      MAR93     sedan        802         4.4682
           9      MAR93     wagon        422         2.3511
          10      APR93     coupe        451         2.5127
          11      APR93     sedan        826         4.6019
          12      APR93     wagon        329         1.8330
          13      MAY93     coupe        373         2.0781
          14      MAY93     sedan        854         4.7579
          15      MAY93     wagon        236         1.3148
          16      JUN93     coupe        360         2.0057
          17      JUN93     sedan        870         4.8471
          18      JUN93     wagon        285         1.5878
          19      JUL93     coupe        349         1.9444
          20      JUL93     sedan        903         5.0309
          21      JUL93     wagon        252         1.4040
          22      AUG93     coupe        356         1.9834
          23      AUG93     sedan        901         5.0198
          24      AUG93     wagon        302         1.6825
          25      SEP93     coupe        316         1.7605
          26      SEP93     sedan        935         5.2092
          27      SEP93     wagon        239         1.3316
          28      OCT93     coupe        309         1.7215
          29      OCT93     sedan        925         5.1535
          30      OCT93     wagon        255         1.4207
          31      NOV93     coupe        293         1.6324
          32      NOV93     sedan        858         4.7802
          33      NOV93     wagon        233         1.2981
          34      DEC93     coupe        256         1.4263
          35      DEC93     sedan        831         4.6298
          36      DEC93     wagon        234         1.3037
```

The crosstabulated car sales data listing in Output 4.4 shows the total number of coupes, sedans, and wagons sold in each month of 1993. The following sections show how to produce useful plots of these data.

Line-Printer Plots Using the PLOT Procedure

Use PROC PLOT to produce line-printer quality graphs of one variable against another. In the following example, you plot the number of cars sold against time to examine the trend in car sales for each style of car. The specification

```
count*pdate=style
```

in the PLOT statement enables you to produce the plot of cars sold (COUNT) against time (PDATE). The values of the STYLE variable mark each point on the plot. The first (left-most) nonblank character in the formatted value of the STYLE variable is used as the plotting symbol. The following example program uses PROC PLOT to produce the plot in Output 4.5:

```
proc plot data=carout;
   plot count*pdate=style;
run;
```

Output 4.5
Plot of Car Sales
Data Using PROC
PLOT

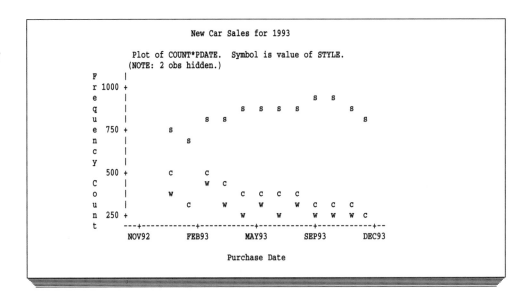

High-Resolution Plots Using the GPLOT Procedure

Use PROC GPLOT to produce high-resolution quality graphs of one variable against another. PROC GPLOT provides you with more features than does PROC PLOT for customizing your plots. As in the previous example, you want to plot the number of cars sold against time to examine the trend in car sales for each style of car.

Use the statements and options described in the following list to produce the graph of car sales for 1993:

GOPTIONS statement
  enables you to specify global options for the graphics environment. In this example, you request that a border be drawn around the graphics output area.

AXIS statements
  define options for the two axes in the plot:

ORDER= option	selects and orders the values for the major tick marks on a plot axis.
MINOR= option	defines the number and appearance of the minor tick marks on an axis.
OFFSET= option	specifies how far to move the first and last major tick marks from each end of the axis line.

| LABEL= option | specifies the text and appearance of the axis label. The ANGLE= option specifies the angle of the entire text string with respect to the horizontal. The ROTATE= option specifies the degree by which to rotate individual characters with respect to the current base line. |

PROC GPLOT statement

invokes the procedure and enables you to specify the input data set in the DATA= option.

SYMBOL statements

specify the characteristics of the symbols that display the data plotted by the GPLOT procedure. Each SYMBOL statement applies to each value of STYLE in alphabetical order. For example, the third SYMBOL statement applies to the third alphabetical value of STYLE, which is `wagon`. In this example, the following options appear in the SYMBOL statements:

I= option	specifies the interpolation method for the data points displayed in the graph. In this example, I=JOIN specifies that a straight line connects the data points.
COLOR= option	specifies a color for the plot symbols and plot lines.
VALUE= option	specifies a plot symbol for the data points.

PLOT statement

creates the plot of the specified variables from the data set specified in the PROC GPLOT statement. In this example, the PLOT statement plots COUNT against PDATE according to the values of STYLE. This produces multiple plots on one set of axes and automatically generates a legend. Use the HAXIS= and VAXIS= options to associate the horizontal and vertical axes, respectively, with previously specified AXIS statements.

Output 4.6 shows the black-and-white version of the graph created by the following program:

```
goptions border;
axis1 order=('01jan93'd to '01jan94'd by month2)
      minor=(number=1)
      offset=(3,3);
axis2 label=(angle=-90 rotate=90 'Quantity');

proc gplot data=carout;
   symbol1 i=join color=cyan value=C;
   symbol2 i=join color=red value=S;
   symbol3 i=join color=green value=W;
   plot count*pdate=style / haxis=axis1 vaxis=axis2;
run;
```

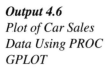

Output 4.6
Plot of Car Sales
Data Using PROC
GPLOT

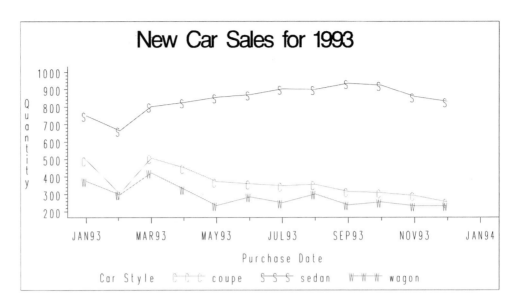

Producing Block, Bar, and Pie Charts

Use the GCHART procedure to produce horizontal or vertical bar charts, block charts, or pie charts of your data. The type of chart you choose to produce depends on the type of information you have and what aspects of the information you want to emphasize. The remaining examples in this chapter use the CARSALES data set containing information on prospective car sales by state and region. The full data set and the DATA step used to create it are shown in the appendix.

Block Chart

The statements and options described in the following list produce a grouped block chart of the prospective car sales data contained in the CARSALES data set:

GOPTIONS statement
> specifies the vertical and horizontal positions with the VPOS= and HPOS= options, respectively, that are necessary to display the full chart.

PROC GCHART statement
> invokes the procedure and enables you to specify the input data set in the DATA= option.

BLOCK statement
> specifies the variable in the input data set with categories of data represented on the chart. Specify the following options in the BLOCK statement:

SUMVAR= option	specifies the variable to be used for sum calculations. Specify TYPE=MEAN to chart the mean statistic instead of the sum.
GROUP= option	in block charts, adds another row or column to the chart to group the data according to values of the specified variable.

In this example, the sum of the QUANTITY variable is displayed on the block chart for each value of the STYLE and REGION variables. Note that the BORDER option is still in effect from the GOPTIONS statement issued previously in the PROC GPLOT example. The following program produces the block chart shown in Output 4.7:

```
goptions vpos=48 hpos=85;

proc gchart data=carsales;
   block style / sumvar=quantity
                 group=region;
run;
```

Output 4.7
Grouped Block
Chart

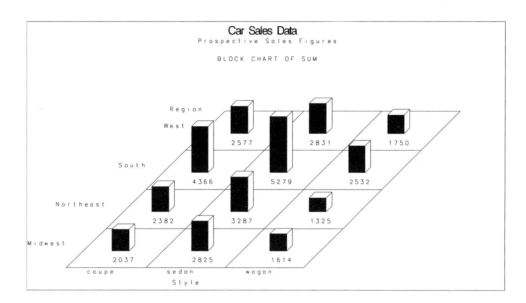

Horizontal Bar Chart

Use PATTERN statements and options in the PROC GCHART step to produce customized horizontal bar charts. PATTERN statements define the characteristics of patterns used in graphs. In this example, you use PATTERN statements to specify fill patterns and colors for the bars in the graph.

Specify the following options in the HBAR statement to produce a subgrouped horizontal bar chart:

SUMVAR= option	specifies the variable to be used for sum or mean calculations. In this example, you compute the sum of the QUANTITY variable.
SUM option	requests that the sum be calculated for the variable specified in the SUMVAR= option.
SUBGROUP= option	divides the bars into segments according to the values of the specified variable. In this example, each bar is divided into three segments, representing the three different values of the STYLE variable.

Output 4.8 shows the black-and-white version of the chart created by the following program:

```
pattern1 value=solid color=cyan;
pattern2 value=x1 color=red;
pattern3 value=empty;

proc gchart data=carsales;
   hbar region / sumvar=quantity
               sum
               subgroup=style;
run;
```

Output 4.8
Horizontal Bar
Chart with
Subgrouping

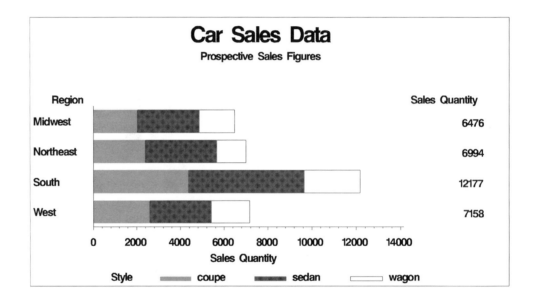

Vertical Bar Chart

You can create a vertical bar chart with subgrouping by using a program similar to the one you used to create the horizontal bar chart. To produce a vertical bar chart, you use a VBAR statement instead of an HBAR statement. Because the PATTERN statements are still in effect from the previous example, you do not need to reissue them. In this example, you also perform the following new tasks:

□ Compute the sum for the REVENUE variable by specifying it in the SUMVAR= option in the VBAR statement.

□ Draw a rectangular frame around the axis area using the FRAME option in the VBAR statement.

□ Add a footnote with the FOOTNOTE statement.

Output 4.9 shows the black-and-white version of the chart created by the following program:

```
proc gchart data=carsales;
   vbar region / sumvar=revenue
                 sum
                 subgroup=style
                 frame;
footnote '(Sales in $1000)';
run;
```

Output 4.9
Vertical Bar Chart
with Subgrouping

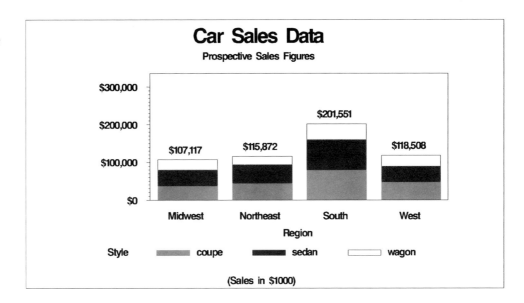

Pie Chart

Use the PIE statement in PROC GCHART to produce pie charts of your data. The following list describes the options used in this example:

SUMVAR= option
    specifies the variable to be used for sum or mean calculations.

SLICE= option
    specifies the method for labeling the name of each slice.

VALUE= option
    specifies the method for labeling the value of the chart statistic for each slice.

PERCENT= option
    prints the percentage of the pie represented by each slice using the specified labeling method.

NOHEADING option
    suppresses the heading normally printed at the top each page or display of pie chart output.

The null FOOTNOTE statement cancels the previous footnote definition.

In this example, the name of each slice is displayed outside the slice, while the value and percentage of the pie represented by each slice are displayed inside each slice. The following program produces the pie chart shown in Output 4.10:

```
proc gchart data=carsales;
   pie region / sumvar=quantity
                slice=outside
                value=inside
                percent=inside
                noheading;
      footnote;
run;
```

Output 4.10
Pie Chart

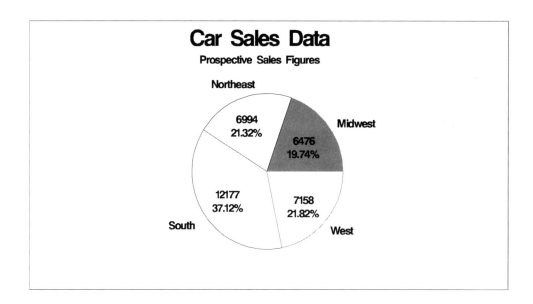

Producing Maps

A map is the best way to represent geographic data. For example, if you have sales information organized by state, country, or region, you can display this information in a map. You can use the GMAP procedure to produce four types of maps: block, choropleth, prism, and surface. This section shows you how to produce block maps and choropleth maps.

To produce a map with the GMAP procedure, you need two SAS data sets: a map data set and a response data set. The *map data set* contains a set of coordinates that represent the boundaries of the map areas; this is the data set that you use to draw the map outlines. The *response data set* contains the data that you want to evaluate and display on the map.

SAS/GRAPH software provides a collection of map data sets. The map data sets should be located in a SAS data library at your site. To determine the name of this SAS data library, consult your SAS Software Consultant.

Once you have located the map data sets, use the following program statement to assign the libref MAPS to the SAS data library:

```
libname maps 'SAS-data-library';
```

Getting the Data into Shape for Mapping

The SAS map data sets for the United States identify states by their two-digit FIPS code. (FIPS is an acronym for Federal Information Processing Standard.) The FIPS code is contained in a variable called STATE in the US map data set. You can use the CONTENTS procedure to find out information such as this about the types of variables in a SAS data set.

For these map examples, you create a new data set, STSALES, from the CARSALES data set. You use STSALES as the response data set. To use the response data set with the map data set, the two data sets must have at least one common ID variable (the same name, length, and type). The following statements create a variable STATE in the new STSALES response data set that contains the state FIPS codes. The STFIPS function converts the two-digit postal abbreviations in the STATENM variable to their corresponding FIPS codes. Thus, STATE is the ID variable linking the response data set, STSALES, to the map data set, US.

```
data stsales;
   set carsales;
   state=stfips(statenm);
run;
```

Block Map

A *block map* is useful for comparing the relative values of a variable across geographic areas. This example shows how to draw a block map for a subset of the full CARSALES data set. The legend is not printed because the purpose of this map is to give a quick and approximate relative comparison of car sales by state. Information on the exact quantities of car sales can be shown in tabular reports, such as those shown previously in this chapter.

Use the statements and options described in the following list to produce a block map of sedan sales quantities for the Midwest sales region:

□ The PATTERN statement specifies the patterns to use in filling the blocks. In this example, you use the VALUE= option to specify a solid fill pattern for all blocks. You can use other options to specify more details about the fill patterns for the blocks.

□ The PROC GMAP statement invokes the procedure and enables you to specify the map and response data sets. Specify the following options in the PROC GMAP statement:

MAP= option   specifies the map data set.

DATA= option   specifies the response data set.

□ The WHERE statement selects only those observations that meet the particular condition specified in the statement. In this example, only observations for sedan sales for states within the Midwest region are selected for mapping.

□ The ID statement specifies the common identification variable shared by the map and response data sets.

□ The BLOCK statement uses the response variable QUANTITY to produce vertical blocks representing the quantity of prospective sedan sales in each state in the Midwest region. Specify the following options in the BLOCK statement:

DISCRETE option   causes the height of each block to represent the individual values of the response variable. By default, the block heights represent midpoints in a range of response variable values.

NOLEGEND option   suppresses the printing of the legend.

□   The FOOTNOTE statement adds a footnote to the map.

The following program produces the block map shown in Output 4.11 (in black-and-white):

```
pattern value=solid;

proc gmap map=maps.us data=stsales;
   where region='Midwest' and style='sedan';
   id state;
   block quantity / discrete nolegend;
   title3 'Midwest Region';
   footnote 'Sedan Sales Quantities';
run;
```

Output 4.11
Block Map

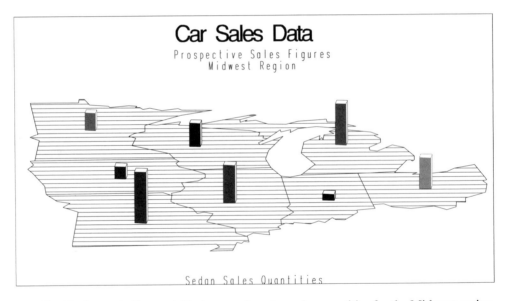

The block map in Output 4.11 shows only sedan sales quantities for the Midwest region because the WHERE statement selected only those observations from the response data set for sedan sales in states within the Midwest sales region. To include the other map areas that do not display data, add the ALL option to the PROC GMAP statement. This option causes PROC GMAP to draw a map of all 50 states but shows data values only for those observations (states) in the response data set that meet the condition specified in the WHERE statement.

Choropleth Map

A *choropleth map* is most useful for highlighting regional differences in the values of a variable. A choropleth map is less useful than a block map in providing a quick comparison of relative values. You almost always need a legend to interpret a choropleth map of a numeric variable.

In the following example, you plot a summarized version of the car sales data to produce a map showing the values of total prospective sales revenue in all 50 states. Before drawing the choropleth map, you first use PROC MEANS to compute a sum for the REVENUE variable in each state. The ID statement writes the specified variable to the output data set.

```
proc means data=stsales noprint;
   by region statenm;
   var revenue;
   id state;
   output out=stsales1 sum=;
run;
```

The previous statements produce an output data set, STSALES1, that contains the total prospective sales revenue for each state. In the STSALES1 data set, the REVENUE variable represents the total value of car sales revenue across all three styles of car (coupe, sedan, and wagon).

The statements and options described in the following list show how to use PROC GMAP to draw a choropleth map for the STSALES1 data set:

□   The PATTERN statements specify the map patterns to fill the map areas. See *SAS/GRAPH Software: Reference* for more information on map patterns.

□   The CHORO statement uses the response variable REVENUE to draw color and pattern combinations representing the values of total prospective car sales revenue in each state. Specify the following options in the CHORO statement:

LEVELS= option	specifies the number of midpoints that the procedure should calculate for values of the response variable. In this example, you specify three levels.
COUTLINE= option	draws an outline in the specified color around each state's borders.

□   The null TITLE3 statement cancels the third line of the title defined in the previous example.

The choropleth map of prospective sales revenue is shown in Output 4.12 (in black-and-white). The map highlights that the eastern states have higher prospective total sales revenues than do nearly all of the western states.

```
pattern1 value=mempty color=white;
pattern2 value=m3n color=cyan;
pattern3 value=m3x color=red;

proc gmap map=maps.us data=stsales1;
   id state;
   choro revenue / levels=3
                   coutline=black;
   title3;
   footnote '(Sales in $1000)';
run;
```

Output 4.12
Choropleth Map

Regional Block Map

A *regional block map* combines features of block maps and choropleth maps to provide information that neither map provides individually. The steps described in the following list describe how to create and process the data sets necessary to produce a regional map for the car sales data:

1. Create a new map data set (called US1 in this example) with a REGION variable that matches the values of the REGION variable in the CARSALES data set. Use the SELECT statement to assign values to the REGION variable based on state FIPS codes:

```
data us1;
   set maps.us;
   select;
      when (state=42 or state=34 or state=36 or
            state=09 or state=44 or state=25 or
            state=50 or state=33 or state=23)
            region='Northeast';
      when (state=27 or state=55 or state=26 or
            state=19 or state=29 or state=17 or
            state=18 or state=39) region='Midwest';
      when (state=21 or state=54 or state=51 or
            state=11 or state=24 or state=10 or
            state=05 or state=47 or state=37 or
            state=45 or state=22 or state=01 or
            state=28 or state=13 or state=12)
            region='South';
      otherwise region='West';
   end;
run;
```

2. Sort the new map data set by the values of REGION and STATE. Use PROC SORT to sort the US1 data set:

```
proc sort data=us1;
   by region state;
run;
```

3. Remove the internal boundary coordinates from the map data set. The GREMOVE procedure uses an input map data set to create a new output map data set with boundary coordinates for the new map areas specified in the BY statement. The boundary coordinates for the map areas specified in the ID statement are removed.

```
proc gremove data=us1 out=us2;
   by region;
   id state;
run;
```

4. Create a summary of the REVENUE variable for each geographic region. Use PROC MEANS on the STSALES data set to create a new data set, STSALES2, containing a variable representing the total sales revenue across all car styles and all states within each region. The STSALES2 data set contains four observations — one for each region.

```
proc means data=stsales noprint;
   by region;
   var revenue;
   output out=stsales2 sum=;
run;
```

5. Draw the regional block map using the US1 data set as the map data set and the STSALES2 data set as the response data set. The AREA= option in the BLOCK statement tells PROC GMAP which variable in the ID statement to use to draw patterns in the map areas. AREA=1 tells PROC GMAP to use the first ID variable to draw map patterns. In this example, REGION is the only ID variable; still, you must use the AREA= option if you want PROC GMAP to draw a different pattern in each region. If you omit the AREA= option, PROC GMAP draws the same pattern in all map areas, thereby making them indistinguishable.

In this example, eight PATTERN statements specify details about the eight different patterns in the map. The first four statements define block patterns, and the last four statements define map patterns.

Output 4.13 shows a black-and-white version of the regional block map produced by the following statements:

```
goptions reset=global border;

pattern1 value=solid color=cyan;
pattern2 value=empty color=green;
pattern3 value=r1 color=red;
pattern4 value=solid color=black;
pattern5 value=m1x color=black;
pattern6 value=m2n color=green;
pattern7 value=m5x color=red;
pattern8 value=m1n color=cyan;
```

```
proc gmap map=us2 data=stsales2;
    id region;
    block revenue / discrete area=1 coutline=black;
    title 'Car Sales Data';
    title2 'Prospective Total Sales Revenue';
    footnote '(Sales in $1000)';
run;
```

Output 4.13
Regional Block Map

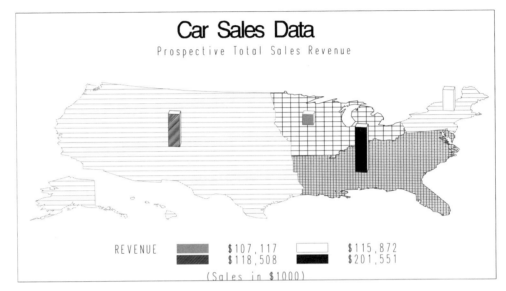

Learning More

☐   For more complete information and more examples on report writing with SAS software, see *Report Writing with SAS Software: Examples, Version 6, First Edition.*

☐   For an introduction to SAS/ASSIST software, see *Getting Started with the SAS System Using SAS/ASSIST Software, Version 6, First Edition.*

☐   For complete reference information on the GCHART, GMAP, GPLOT, and GREMOVE procedures and other details on SAS/GRAPH software, see *SAS/GRAPH Software: Reference, Version 6, First Edition, Volume 1* and *Volume 2.*

☐   For more information about map data sets, see SAS Technical Report P-196, *SAS/GRAPH Software: Map Data Sets, Release 6.06.*

☐   For complete reference information on the CONTENTS, FREQ, MEANS, PLOT, PRINT, and SORT procedures, see the *SAS Procedures Guide, Version 6, Third Edition.*

☐   For complete reference and usage information on PROC REPORT, see the *SAS Guide to the REPORT Procedure: Usage and Reference, Version 6, First Edition* and SAS Technical Report P-258, *Using the REPORT Procedure in a Nonwindowing Environment, Release 6.07.*

☐   For complete reference and usage information on PROC TABULATE, see the *SAS Guide to TABULATE Processing, Second Edition.*

Chapter 5 Analyzing Qualitative Marketing Data

Introduction

This chapter shows how to create tables for and analyze the type of marketing data that can be classified as qualitative frequency data. Survey data for which the responses fall into unordered categories, such as names, abstract concepts, or sensory perceptions (flavors, smells, and so on) can be classified as qualitative data. Data measured in this way are called *nominal* data. Some marketing data with an inherent ordering, referred to as *ordinal* data, can also sometimes be classified as qualitative. Data can be treated as if they were qualitative if the data variables have a small number of levels, regardless of how the data are measured. In contrast, quantitative data always have at least an inherent ordering, and quantitative variables typically have a large number of different levels. The types of analyses that are valid and relevant for qualitative data are usually different from those for quantitative data. For more information on the distinction between qualitative and quantitative data and for information on measurement levels, see Chapter 1, "Introduction."

In this chapter, you see how to produce crosstabulation tables for survey responses or other types of qualitative marketing data. You also learn how to perform some relevant analyses for the data in these tables. Among other factors, the type of analysis you perform depends on the size of the table and whether the data have been divided into groups.

Chapter 6, "Analyzing Quantitative Marketing Data," explains how to perform statistical analyses on marketing data that can be classified as quantitative.

SAS Data Example

Suppose you have data from a survey of potential car buyers. In this chapter, you want to analyze the responses to one set of questions from the survey that pertain to the most important factors buyers use in choosing which car to buy. A question on the survey asks what factor, other than price, is the most important in deciding which car to buy. The choices are

□   safety

□   reliability

□   performance

□   unknown/other.

You have a portion of the data from the survey in a SAS data set called CARFACS, organized as follows:

```
AGEGRP FACTOR        PURCH3
3      reliability   N
1      performance   Y
3      safety        N
4      performance   Y
5      unknown/other N
more SAS data lines
```

□   AGEGRP is a numeric variable that describes the age category of the survey respondents. AGEGRP is formatted with a user-defined format called AGEFMT, as follows:

1=18-24

2=25-34

3=35-44

4=45-54

5=55+

See the *SAS Procedures Guide* for information on using the FORMAT procedure to create formats for variables.

□   FACTOR is a variable that describes the most important factor, other than price, that the survey respondent uses to decide which car to buy.

□   PURCH3 is a variable that tells whether the respondent has purchased a car in the last three years (Y=Yes, N=No).

The following SAS statements print the first five observations of the CARFACS data set in Output 5.1:

```
/* Global Title Statement */
title 'Car Survey Data';

proc print data=carfacs(obs=5);
run;
```

Output 5.1
Partial Listing of
CARFACS Data Set

```
                        Car Survey Data

           OBS    FACTOR          AGEGRP    PURCH3

            1     reliability     35-44      N
            2     performance     18-24      Y
            3     safety          35-44      N
            4     performance     45-54      Y
            5     unknown/other   55+        N
```

Producing Crosstabulation Tables

The FREQ procedure provides a simple way to produce crosstabulation tables. Suppose you want to examine the relationship between age and factors influencing car purchases. Use PROC FREQ to create a two-way crosstabulation table for these two variables. The SAS statements described in the following list create a two-way crosstabulation table of FACTOR by AGEGRP. By default, PROC FREQ orders the data by their unformatted values.

PROC FREQ statement
> invokes the procedure and enables you to specify options for the PROC FREQ step. The DATA= option specifies the input data set.

TABLES statement
> specifies the crosstabulation or frequency table requests, where each request consists of one or more variable names joined by asterisks. When you join two variables with an asterisk you create a two-way crosstabulation table, where the values of the first variable form the rows of the table, and the values of the second variable form the columns of the table.

The following SAS statements produce the table shown in Output 5.2:

```
proc freq data=carfacs;
   tables factor*agegrp;
run;
```

Output 5.2
Crosstabulation
Table of FACTOR
by AGEGRP

```
                               Car Survey Data

                            TABLE OF FACTOR BY AGEGRP

           FACTOR        AGEGRP

           Frequency  |
           Percent    |
           Row Pct    |
           Col Pct    |18-24   |25-34   |35-44   |45-54   |55+     |  Total
           -----------+--------+--------+--------+--------+--------+
           performance |     16 |      8 |     10 |      6 |      5 |     45
                       |   9.82 |   4.91 |   6.13 |   3.68 |   3.07 |  27.61
                       |  35.56 |  17.78 |  22.22 |  13.33 |  11.11 |
                       |  48.48 |  25.81 |  30.30 |  16.67 |  16.67 |
           -----------+--------+--------+--------+--------+--------+
           reliability |      5 |      9 |      9 |     12 |     13 |     48
                       |   3.07 |   5.52 |   5.52 |   7.36 |   7.98 |  29.45
                       |  10.42 |  18.75 |  18.75 |  25.00 |  27.08 |
                       |  15.15 |  29.03 |  27.27 |  33.33 |  43.33 |
           -----------+--------+--------+--------+--------+--------+
           safety      |      8 |     12 |     11 |     14 |      9 |     54
                       |   4.91 |   7.36 |   6.75 |   8.59 |   5.52 |  33.13
                       |  14.81 |  22.22 |  20.37 |  25.93 |  16.67 |
                       |  24.24 |  38.71 |  33.33 |  38.89 |  30.00 |
           -----------+--------+--------+--------+--------+--------+
           unknown/other |    4 |      2 |      3 |      4 |      3 |     16
                       |   2.45 |   1.23 |   1.84 |   2.45 |   1.84 |   9.82
                       |  25.00 |  12.50 |  18.75 |  25.00 |  18.75 |
                       |  12.12 |   6.45 |   9.09 |  11.11 |  10.00 |
           -----------+--------+--------+--------+--------+--------+
           Total            33       31       33       36       30      163
                         20.25    19.02    20.25    22.09    18.40   100.00
```

Interpretation of output

The crosstabulation table in Output 5.2 contains one cell for each combination of age group and factor. By default, each cell contains four statistics:

Frequency
> is a count of the number of observations from the input data set that have the indicated values of the two variables.

Percent
> is the percentage of the total frequency count represented by that cell.

Row Pct
> is the row percentage, the percentage of the total frequency count for that row represented by the cell.

Col Pct
> is the column percentage, the percentage of the total frequency count for that column represented by the cell.

You can suppress the printing of the statistics by specifying the NOFREQ, NOPERCENT, NOROW, and NOCOL options after a slash (/) in the TABLES statement. You can store the frequency counts and cell percentages in an output data set by specifying the name of the data set in the OUT= option in the TABLES statement.

Total frequency counts and percentages for each row, each column, and the entire table are printed around the edges of the table.

Creating Multiple Crosstabulation Tables

With PROC FREQ, you can create as many crosstabulation tables as you want by joining more variables with asterisks in the TABLES statement. The last two variables listed in the TABLES statement define the rows and columns of a two-way table that is produced for each combination of levels of the previous variables in the list.

In this example, you add PURCH3 to the beginning of the list of variables in the TABLES statement. PURCH3 has two levels, N and Y, so specifying PURCH3*FACTOR*AGEGRP in the TABLES statement produces two two-way crosstabulation tables.

The following SAS statements produce the two tables shown in Output 5.3:

```
proc freq data=carfacs;
   tables purch3*factor*agegrp;
run;
```

Output 5.3
Multiple Crosstabulation Tables of FACTOR by AGEGRP

```
                              Car Survey Data                            1

                         TABLE 1 OF FACTOR BY AGEGRP
                          CONTROLLING FOR PURCH3=N

        FACTOR         AGEGRP

        Frequency  |
        Percent    |
        Row Pct    |
        Col Pct    |18-24   |25-34   |35-44   |45-54   |55+     | Total
        -----------+--------+--------+--------+--------+--------+
        performance|     4  |     2  |     2  |     2  |     2  |    12
                   |  4.65  |  2.33  |  2.33  |  2.33  |  2.33  | 13.95
                   | 33.33  | 16.67  | 16.67  | 16.67  | 16.67  |
                   | 28.57  | 12.50  | 11.76  | 11.11  |  9.52  |
        -----------+--------+--------+--------+--------+--------+
        reliability|     3  |     7  |     6  |     6  |    10  |    32
                   |  3.49  |  8.14  |  6.98  |  6.98  | 11.63  | 37.21
                   |  9.38  | 21.88  | 18.75  | 18.75  | 31.25  |
                   | 21.43  | 43.75  | 35.29  | 33.33  | 47.62  |
        -----------+--------+--------+--------+--------+--------+
        safety     |     5  |     7  |     7  |     9  |     7  |    35
                   |  5.81  |  8.14  |  8.14  | 10.47  |  8.14  | 40.70
                   | 14.29  | 20.00  | 20.00  | 25.71  | 20.00  |
                   | 35.71  | 43.75  | 41.18  | 50.00  | 33.33  |
        -----------+--------+--------+--------+--------+--------+
        unknown/other|   2  |     0  |     2  |     1  |     2  |     7
                   |  2.33  |  0.00  |  2.33  |  1.16  |  2.33  |  8.14
                   | 28.57  |  0.00  | 28.57  | 14.29  | 28.57  |
                   | 14.29  |  0.00  | 11.76  |  5.56  |  9.52  |
        -----------+--------+--------+--------+--------+--------+
        Total            14       16       17       18       21       86
                      16.28    18.60    19.77    20.93    24.42   100.00
```

```
                              Car Survey Data                              2

                         TABLE 2 OF FACTOR BY AGEGRP
                           CONTROLLING FOR PURCH3=Y

         FACTOR         AGEGRP

         Frequency   |
         Percent     |
         Row Pct     |
         Col Pct     |18-24  |25-34  |35-44  |45-54  |55+    | Total
         ------------+-------+-------+-------+-------+-------+
         performance |    12 |     6 |     8 |     4 |     3 |    33
                     | 15.58 |  7.79 | 10.39 |  5.19 |  3.90 | 42.86
                     | 36.36 | 18.18 | 24.24 | 12.12 |  9.09 |
                     | 63.16 | 40.00 | 50.00 | 22.22 | 33.33 |
         ------------+-------+-------+-------+-------+-------+
         reliability |     2 |     2 |     3 |     6 |     3 |    16
                     |  2.60 |  2.60 |  3.90 |  7.79 |  3.90 | 20.78
                     | 12.50 | 12.50 | 18.75 | 37.50 | 18.75 |
                     | 10.53 | 13.33 | 18.75 | 33.33 | 33.33 |
         ------------+-------+-------+-------+-------+-------+
         safety      |     3 |     5 |     4 |     5 |     2 |    19
                     |  3.90 |  6.49 |  5.19 |  6.49 |  2.60 | 24.68
                     | 15.79 | 26.32 | 21.05 | 26.32 | 10.53 |
                     | 15.79 | 33.33 | 25.00 | 27.78 | 22.22 |
         ------------+-------+-------+-------+-------+-------+
         unknown/other|    2 |     2 |     1 |     3 |     1 |     9
                     |  2.60 |  2.60 |  1.30 |  3.90 |  1.30 | 11.69
                     | 22.22 | 22.22 | 11.11 | 33.33 | 11.11 |
                     | 10.53 | 13.33 |  6.25 | 16.67 | 11.11 |
         ------------+-------+-------+-------+-------+-------+
         Total            19      15      16      18       9      77
                        24.68   19.48   20.78   23.38   11.69  100.00
```

The first table in Output 5.3 shows the crosstabulation of factor by age group among those who have not purchased a car within the past three years. The second table shows the crosstabulation for those who have purchased a car within the past three years.

Analyzing Crosstabulation Tables

The appropriate test or measure of association for your data depends on the type of data you are analyzing. For more information to help you decide which tests and measures to use for a specific set of data, see Hays (1981). You can use PROC FREQ to produce different tests and measures of association depending on whether the crosstabulation table is a 2 × 2 table or a larger (r × c) table and whether the data are *stratified*. You stratify data when you divide it into two or more groups (or blocks). *Stratified analysis* is a method of adjusting for the effect of other variables without needing to estimate parameters for them.

Measures of Association for a Single r × c Table

Specify the MEASURES option after a slash (/) in the TABLES statement to print a list of tests and measures of association in the PROC FREQ output. The NOPRINT option in the TABLES statement suppresses printing of the crosstabulation table but allows printing of the statistics. The examples in this section use the CARFACS data set containing car-purchase survey information. The following SAS code produces the statistics shown in Output 5.4:

```
proc freq data=carfacs;
   tables factor*agegrp / measures noprint;
run;
```

Output 5.4
Measures of
Association for an
r × c Table

```
                          Car Survey Data

              STATISTICS FOR TABLE OF FACTOR BY AGEGRP

       Statistic                        Value      ASE
       ------------------------------------------------
       Gamma                            -0.136     0.084
       Kendall's Tau-b                  -0.104     0.064
       Stuart's Tau-c                   -0.105     0.065

       Somers' D C|R                    -0.110     0.068
       Somers' D R|C                    -0.098     0.061

       Pearson Correlation              -0.123     0.078
       Spearman Correlation             -0.127     0.078

       Lambda Asymmetric C|R             0.087     0.052
       Lambda Asymmetric R|C             0.110     0.059
       Lambda Symmetric                  0.097     0.050

       Uncertainty Coefficient C|R       0.028     0.014
       Uncertainty Coefficient R|C       0.034     0.018
       Uncertainty Coefficient Symmetric 0.031     0.016

       Sample Size = 163
```

Interpreting the Statistics

PROC FREQ produces a list of 13 statistics and their asymptotic standard errors (ASE) in the output when you specify the MEASURES option in the TABLES statement. The first seven statistics listed in Output 5.4 are based on the assumption that both variables in the two-way table have an inherent ordering. That is, the first seven statistics are valid only if both variables are measured on an ordinal scale. Because the FACTOR variable is a nominal variable, these statistics are not valid for this example. For complete reference information on the statistics produced by PROC FREQ, see the *SAS Procedures Guide*.

The lambda coefficients and the uncertainty coefficients are the measures of association to use if at least one of the variables in the two-way table is nominally scaled. They have a range between zero and one. The higher the value of the coefficient, the higher the level of association between the two variables in the table. Choose the coefficient you want to use according to its interpretation, described in the following sections.

Each measure has three forms:

C | R
   treats the column variable as the dependent, or response, variable and the row variable as the fixed variable with known values.

R | C
   treats the row variable as the dependent variable and the column variable as fixed.

Symmetric

is the symmetric version of the previous two measures. For the lambda coefficient, the symmetric coefficient is a simple average of the two asymmetric coefficients. For the uncertainty coefficient, the symmetric coefficient is a more complicated combination of the two asymmetric coefficients.

The Lambda Coefficient

The *lambda coefficient* is defined as the proportional reduction of the expected number of predictive errors gained by knowledge of the independent variable. That is,

$$\lambda(Y|X) = \frac{\textit{the reduction in the expected number of errors gained by knowing X}}{\textit{the expected number of errors given no knowledge of X}} \quad .$$

For the crosstabulation table shown in Output 5.2, knowledge of AGEGRP enables you to reduce the expected number of errors you would make in predicting the value of FACTOR. If you had no knowledge of AGEGRP, your best guess of FACTOR would be `safety` because 54 people in your survey chose safety as their primary factor in choosing a car. Your survey respondents chose safety more often than any other factor, yet 109 people chose other factors. Thus, if you predict that safety is the most important factor, you make 109 predictive errors.

When you look at the crosstabulation of AGEGRP by FACTOR, you can see that for the 18-24 age group and the 55+ age group safety was not the primary factor. For the 18-24 age group, 16 people chose performance as the primary factor, while only 8 chose safety. For the 55+ age group, 13 people chose reliability as the primary factor, while only 9 chose safety. Knowing the breakdown by age group enables you to make 12([16 − 8]+[13 − 9]) fewer predictive errors. Thus, for the two-way table of AGEGRP by FACTOR, the lambda(R | C) coefficient is calculated as follows:

$$\lambda(R|C) = 12 / 109 = .11 \quad .$$

You can make similar calculations for the lambda(C | R) coefficient. The symmetric lambda coefficient is the average of the two asymmetric coefficients.

The Uncertainty Coefficient

To understand the uncertainty coefficient, you must first understand the concept of *entropy*. Entropy is a measure of variability for nominal data. Entropy is minimized (to 0) when all the data are in a single category of the dependent variable. It is maximized when the data are spread out evenly in all of the categories of the dependent variable. The overall entropy in the dependent variable can be expressed by the following equation involving a natural log, where the dependent variable, Y, has proportions, p_i, corresponding to its q different response levels.

$$H(Y) = \sum_{i=1}^{q} p_i \, log\left(1 / p_i\right)$$

When p_i is 0, then $p_i \, log \, (1/p_i)$ is defined as 0.

You can also measure the amount of entropy in the dependent variable for each level of the independent variable using a similar formula. You can define the average amount of entropy for the dependent variable, Y, for each level of the independent variable, X, as follows:

$$H_x(Y) = \textit{the average amount of entropy in the dependent variable}$$
$$\textit{for each level of the independent variable} \quad .$$

The *uncertainty coefficient* is defined as the proportion of the entropy in the dependent variable that is explained by the independent variable. That is,

$$U(C|R) = \frac{H(Y) - H_X(Y)}{H(Y)}$$

where Y is the column variable and X is the row variable. You can calculate the uncertainty coefficient, $U(R \mid C)$, by interchanging the Y and X in the preceding formula.

The symmetric version of the uncertainty coefficient is a combined measure of the two asymmetric versions, as expressed by the following equation:

$$U(Symmetric) = \frac{H(Y) - H_X(Y) + H(X) - H_Y(X)}{H(Y) + H(X)} \quad .$$

Measures of Association for a Single 2 × 2 Table

Two measures of association are commonly computed for 2 × 2 tables:

□ relative risk

□ odds ratios.

When you collect data prospectively (with the predictor variable measured before the outcome variable), the study is sometimes called a *cohort study*. For cohort studies, you compute the relative risk, which is defined as

$$\frac{Prob\{Outcome = Yes|Predictor = Yes\}}{Prob\{Outcome = Yes|Predictor = No\}} \quad .$$

Relative risk is a common measure in the health sciences but is applicable to other areas as well. It ranges from zero to infinity, with values greater than 1 representing a higher likelihood of being in the positive ('Yes') category for the response variable, given that the predictor variable is also positive.

When you collect data retrospectively (with the outcome variable measured before the predictor variable), the study is sometimes called a *case-control study*. For case-control studies, you compute the *odds ratio*, which is actually an estimator of the relative risk for rare events (approximately $p<0.1$). The odds ratio is defined computationally as

$$OR = (n11 \times n22) / (n12 \times n21)$$

where $n11$, $n12$, $n21$, and $n22$ correspond to the four cells of the 2 × 2 table, as shown here:

n11	n12
n21	n22

Calculating Relative Risk

Suppose you want to study the effect of a coupon promotion on purchases of new cars at your dealership. You send one group of 60 potential customers a rebate coupon, and you send a separate group of 60 customers just an invitation to visit your dealership. Then, you track the sales made to customers receiving coupons and those not receiving coupons over the next year. At the end of one year, you have four groups of customers in your study:

1. Customers received a coupon and used it on the purchase of a new car.

2. Customers received a coupon but did not purchase a new car.

3. Customers received only an invitation (no coupon) and purchased a new car.

4. Customers received only an invitation and did not purchase a new car.

Instead of entering single observations for each customer in the study, you enter a variable, COUNT, containing the total number of responses that fall into each of the four categories.

The following SAS code shows how you can enter this information into a SAS data set, CARSALES:

```
data carsales;
   input coupon $ purchase $ count;
   cards;
Y Y 13
Y N 47
N Y 4
N N 56
;
```

For this example, if people who receive the coupon are more likely to buy cars than people who do not receive the coupon, then the relative risk will be significantly greater than 1.

The following example uses PROC FREQ to calculate relative risk, with these statements and options specified:

□   To give you the expected results, you should have the cell corresponding to ('Yes', 'Yes') be the upper left or (1,1) cell in the table. The ORDER=DATA specification in the PROC FREQ statement orders the data the same way that they are ordered in the input data set. If you change the ordering of the input data set by sorting it, for example, then you will get incorrect results.

□   The NOPERCENT, NOROW, and NOCOL options in the TABLE statement suppress the printing of the cell percentages, row percentages, and column percentages in the two-way crosstabulation table. In this example, only the cell frequencies are displayed in the table.

□   The WEIGHT statement identifies the variable in the input data set used to weight each cell of the table.

The results are shown in Output 5.5.

```
proc freq data=carsales order=data;
   tables coupon*purchase / measures
                            nopercent
                            norow
                            nocol;
   weight count;
run;
```

Output 5.5
Relative Risk
Measures for a
2 × 2 Table

```
                        Car Survey Data

                TABLE OF COUPON BY PURCHASE

        COUPON     PURCHASE

        Frequency|Y       |N       | Total
        ---------+--------+--------+
        Y        |   13 |   47 |    60
        ---------+--------+--------+
        N        |    4 |   56 |    60
        ---------+--------+--------+
        Total        17      103     120


          STATISTICS FOR TABLE OF COUPON BY PURCHASE

        Statistic                        Value      ASE
        -------------------------------------------------
        Gamma                            0.590    0.197
        Kendall's Tau-b                  0.215    0.082
        Stuart's Tau-c                   0.150    0.062

        Somers' D C|R                    0.150    0.062
        Somers' D R|C                    0.308    0.114

        Pearson Correlation              0.215    0.082
        Spearman Correlation             0.215    0.082

        Lambda Asymmetric C|R            0.000    0.000
        Lambda Asymmetric R|C            0.150    0.156
        Lambda Symmetric                 0.117    0.124

        Uncertainty Coefficient C|R      0.059    0.046
        Uncertainty Coefficient R|C      0.035    0.028
        Uncertainty Coefficient Symmetric 0.044   0.034


           Estimates of the Relative Risk (Row1/Row2)

                                         95%
        Type of Study      Value    Confidence Bounds
        --------------------------------------------------
        Case-Control       3.872    1.183    12.676
        Cohort (Col1 Risk) 3.250    1.124     9.399
        Cohort (Col2 Risk) 0.839    0.723     0.974


        Sample Size = 120
```

Interpretation of output

Measures of relative risk are listed in the table labeled "Estimates of the Relative Risk (Row1/Row2)," near the bottom of the output. In this example, you are interested in the likelihood that the customer will purchase a car. The 'Yes' value for this question is in column 1 of the crosstabulation table, so you are interested in the value labeled "Cohort (Col1 Risk)." This value is 3.250 with 95% confidence bounds of 1.124 and 9.399. You can conclude that a person who receives a rebate coupon is about 3.25 times as likely to purchase a car from your dealership as a person who does not receive a rebate coupon. In other words, the rebate coupon promotion is effective in increasing car sales. The profitability of using rebate coupons to increase sales is a separate issue that can be analyzed in other ways.

Calculating Odds Ratios

Suppose you take a random sample of your customers who have purchased a car from your dealership and ask them if they own a boat. Then, you ask the same question of a representative sample of noncustomers. The purpose of this survey is to determine if boat ownership is a predictor of car purchase. This is a retrospective study, as you collect the predictor variable (boat ownership) after collecting the response variable (car purchase). This is a case-control study, with your customers composing the cases and the noncustomers composing the controls.

The following SAS statements show how you can enter this information into a SAS data set, CARBOATS:

```
data carboats;
   input type $ boat $ count;
   cards;
case Y 6
case N 54
control Y 5
control N 55
;
```

For this example, if people who own boats are more likely than people who do not own boats to purchase a car from your dealership, then the odds ratio will be significantly greater than 1.

The following SAS statements use PROC FREQ to display the crosstabulation table and compute the odds ratio for the CARBOATS data set. The results are shown in Output 5.6.

```
proc freq data=carboats order=data;
   tables type*boat / measures
                      nopercent
                      norow
                      nocol;
   weight count;
run;
```

Output 5.6
Odds Ratio
Measures for a
2 × 2 Table

```
                         Car Survey Data

                      TABLE OF TYPE BY BOAT

            TYPE      BOAT

            Frequency|Y        |N        | Total
            ---------+---------+---------+
            case     |    6 |     54 |     60
            ---------+---------+---------+
            control  |    5 |     55 |     60
            ---------+---------+---------+
            Total         11       109      120


                 STATISTICS FOR TABLE OF TYPE BY BOAT

            Statistic                        Value      ASE
            -----------------------------------------------------
            Gamma                            0.100      0.314
            Kendall's Tau-b                  0.029      0.091
            Stuart's Tau-c                   0.017      0.053

            Somers' D C|R                    0.017      0.053
            Somers' D R|C                    0.050      0.158

            Pearson Correlation              0.029      0.091
            Spearman Correlation             0.029      0.091

            Lambda Asymmetric C|R            0.000      0.000
            Lambda Asymmetric R|C            0.017      0.173
            Lambda Symmetric                 0.014      0.146

            Uncertainty Coefficient C|R      0.001      0.009
            Uncertainty Coefficient R|C      0.001      0.004
            Uncertainty Coefficient Symmetric 0.001     0.005


                Estimates of the Relative Risk (Row1/Row2)

                                             95%
            Type of Study        Value    Confidence Bounds
            -----------------------------------------------------
            Case-Control         1.222    0.352      4.244
            Cohort (Col1 Risk)   1.200    0.387      3.721
            Cohort (Col2 Risk)   0.982    0.876      1.100


            Sample Size = 120
```

Interpretation of output

The odds ratio for these data is listed in the table labeled "Estimates of the Relative Risk (Row1/Row2)," near the bottom of the output. In this example, you are interested in the value labeled Case-Control. This value is 1.222, with 95% confidence bounds of 0.352 and 4.244. Although the estimated odds ratio is greater than 1, the lower 95% confidence bound is less than 1. Thus, you cannot conclude (at the 95% confidence level) that boat owners are more likely than other people to purchase cars from your dealership.

For more information on relative risk and odds ratios, see Breslow (1982), Breslow and Day (1980), Fleiss (1981), and Kleinbaum et al (1982).

Tests of No Association for a Single r × c Table

You can use PROC FREQ to perform statistical tests of no association. The null hypothesis of this test is that there is no association between the row variable and the column variable. The chi-square test of no association measures the strength of the evidence that an association exists, not the strength of the association.

To calculate tests of no association, include the CHISQ option in the TABLES statement of PROC FREQ, as shown in the following example for the CARFACS data set. The resulting table and statistics are shown in Output 5.7.

```
proc freq data=carfacs;
    tables factor*agegrp / nopercent
                           nocol
                           norow
                           chisq;
run;
```

Output 5.7
Tests of No
Association for an
r × c Table

```
                              Car Survey Data

                        TABLE OF FACTOR BY AGEGRP

        FACTOR        AGEGRP

        Frequency    |18-24  |25-34  |35-44  |45-54  |55+    |  Total
        -------------+-------+-------+-------+-------+-------+
        performance  |   16  |    8  |   10  |    6  |    5  |    45
        -------------+-------+-------+-------+-------+-------+
        reliability  |    5  |    9  |    9  |   12  |   13  |    48
        -------------+-------+-------+-------+-------+-------+
        safety       |    8  |   12  |   11  |   14  |    9  |    54
        -------------+-------+-------+-------+-------+-------+
        unknown/other|    4  |    2  |    3  |    4  |    3  |    16
        -------------+-------+-------+-------+-------+-------+
        Total            33      31      33      36      30      163


                 STATISTICS FOR TABLE OF FACTOR BY AGEGRP

        Statistic                   DF     Value      Prob
        --------------------------------------------------------
        Chi-Square                  12     14.833     0.251
        Likelihood Ratio Chi-Square 12     14.668     0.260
        Mantel-Haenszel Chi-Square   1      2.655     0.103
        Phi Coefficient                     0.302
        Contingency Coefficient             0.289
        Cramer's V                          0.174

        Sample Size = 163
        WARNING:  25% of the cells have expected counts less
                  than 5. Chi-Square may not be a valid test.
```

Interpretation of output

When you specify the CHISQ option in the TABLES statement, PROC FREQ produces a table of statistics listing the degrees of freedom (if relevant), value, and p-value (if relevant) for each statistic. The first two statistics listed in Output 5.7 are the Pearson Chi-Square statistic (labeled simply as Chi-Square) and the Likelihood Ratio Chi-Square statistic. These two statistics require no restrictions on the scale of measurement of the row or column variable. If they are statistically significant, they indicate the presence of a general association between the row variable and the column variable. The Mantel-Haenszel Chi-Square statistic requires that the data be measured on an ordinal scale. It is sensitive only to linear association between the row and column variables.

For these data, none of the Chi-Square statistics are statistically significant at the .05 level. You can conclude that no association exists between the row and column variables.

PROC FREQ issues a warning when the expected counts are less than 5 in 25% or more of the table because the chi-square test may be invalid under those conditions. In this example, the expected counts are less than 5 for the unknown/other category. Use your judgment and experience to decide whether to use the chi-square test when the expected counts are less than 5 in some cells of the table.

For more information on the statistics produced by PROC FREQ, see the *SAS Procedures Guide* or the *SAS/STAT User's Guide.*

Tests of No Association for a Single 2 × 2 Table

For 2 × 2 tables, Fisher's exact test provides a test of no association. Fisher's exact test yields the probability of observing a table that gives at least as much evidence of association as the one actually observed, given that the null hypothesis is true. PROC FREQ calculates Fisher's exact test for any 2 × 2 table when you specify the CHISQ option in the TABLES statement, as shown in the following example for the CARSALES data set. The resulting table and statistics are shown in Output 5.8.

```
proc freq data=carsales order=data;
   tables coupon*purchase / nopercent
                            nocol
                            norow
                            chisq;
   weight count;
run;
```

Output 5.8
Tests of No
Association for a
2 × 2 Table

```
                              Car Survey Data

                      TABLE OF COUPON BY PURCHASE

          COUPON      PURCHASE

          Frequency|Y        |N       | Total
          ---------+--------+--------+
          Y        |   13 |   47 |     60
          ---------+--------+--------+
          N        |    4 |   56 |     60
          ---------+--------+--------+
          Total         17      103     120


                 STATISTICS FOR TABLE OF COUPON BY PURCHASE

          Statistic                    DF     Value     Prob
          ----------------------------------------------------
          Chi-Square                    1     5.551     0.018
          Likelihood Ratio Chi-Square   1     5.804     0.016
          Continuity Adj. Chi-Square    1     4.386     0.036
          Mantel-Haenszel Chi-Square    1     5.505     0.019
          Fisher's Exact Test (Left)                   0.996
                              (Right)                  0.017
                              (2-Tail)                 0.034
          Phi Coefficient                     0.215
          Contingency Coefficient             0.210
          Cramer's V                          0.215

          Sample Size = 120
```

Interpretation of output

PROC FREQ produces three versions of Fisher's exact test:

□ a left-tail test

□ a right-tail test

□ a two-tail test.

The appropriate test depends upon the hypothesis you are testing. For the CARSALES data, for example, if you want to test the hypothesis that coupons increase car sales, then you want to use a right-tail test. A left-tail test is appropriate if you want to test the hypothesis that coupons decrease car sales. A two-tail test is appropriate when you want to test if coupons have any effect on car sales, without assuming that the effect is in one direction or the other.

For the CARSALES data, the right-tail Fisher's exact test has a probability of .017. You can conclude (at the .05 significance level) that customers who receive a rebate coupon are more likely to purchase a car than are customers who do not receive a coupon.

Note: You can also use PROC FREQ to compute a two-tail Fisher's exact test for tables larger than 2 × 2, but it may require very large amounts of CPU time. As the sample size increases per degree of freedom, the test becomes less and less feasible.

For more information on Fisher's exact test, see the *SAS Procedures Guide* or the *SAS/STAT User's Guide*.

Stratified Analysis for r × c Tables

When you divide your data into groups or blocks and can produce individual crosstabulation tables for each group, then you have stratified your data. For example, you can divide the car survey data into two groups — those who have purchased a car within the past three years and those who have not. The survey responses may be different for the two groups. Stratification can help you identify which group or groups of data are responsible for the association between variables. To analyze stratified data, you can examine each table separately, and you can examine summary statistics that explain your data across all strata. Previous sections in this chapter have described ways of analyzing individual tables. This section shows how to use summary statistics to analyze stratified data.

Cochran-Mantel-Haenszel (CMH) statistics are tests of no *partial association*. That is, they test the null hypothesis that there is no association between the row variable and the column variable in any of the strata. PROC FREQ produces three CMH statistics for r × c tables, each with a different alternative hypothesis. These tests are especially sensitive to association when the direction of the association is similar in all strata. In the output of PROC FREQ, these three tests are labeled according to their alternative hypotheses, as follows:

Nonzero Correlation
> is a one degree-of-freedom test, popularized by Mantel and Haenszel (1959) and Mantel (1963). This test is sensitive only to linear association, where the association is in the same direction in each stratum. It is appropriate only when both the row variable and the column variable are ordinally scaled; otherwise, it is meaningless.

Row Mean Scores Differ
> is similar to an analysis-of-variance F statistic with $r - 1$ degrees of freedom, where r is the number of rows in the table. This statistic is sensitive to different mean scores among the r groups of interest. It requires only that the column variable be ordinally scaled.

General Association
> is a generalization of the Pearson chi-square with $(r - 1)*(c - 1)$ degrees of freedom. It is sensitive to general patterns of association in at least one stratum. This test is always interpretable because it does not require an ordinal scale for either variable in the table.

When you use a CMH statistic that assumes one or both variables are measured on an ordinal scale, then PROC FREQ computes scores for the values of the variables. By default, PROC FREQ assigns *table scores* to the values in your tables. Table scores reflect the observed headings of numeric variables in the table or the internal values of formatted variables. If the variables are character, then integer scores are used. You can specify other types of scoring methods in the SCORES= option in the TABLES statement. For more information, see Chapter 23, "The FREQ Procedure," in the *SAS/STAT User's Guide*.

The following example shows how to use PROC FREQ to calculate summary statistics for the CARFACS data. The data are stratified by the two values of the PURCH3 variable. One group of people have purchased a car within the past three years, and the other group of people have not purchased a car within the past three years.

The CMH option in the TABLES statement computes the CMH statistics.[*] The NOPRINT option suppresses printing of the crosstabulation tables. Only the summary statistics are shown in Output 5.9.

```
proc freq data=carfacs;
   tables purch3*factor*agegrp / cmh noprint;
run;
```

Output 5.9
Summary Statistics
for r × c Tables

```
                            Car Survey Data

                 SUMMARY STATISTICS FOR FACTOR BY AGEGRP
                       CONTROLLING FOR PURCH3


        Cochran-Mantel-Haenszel Statistics (Based on Table Scores)

        Statistic   Alternative Hypothesis    DF    Value    Prob
        ---------------------------------------------------------------
            1       Nonzero Correlation        1    1.716    0.190
            2       Row Mean Scores Differ     3    7.963    0.047
            3       General Association       12   12.384    0.415

        Total Sample Size = 163
```

Interpretation of output

In this example, because only the column variable is ordinally scaled, you should ignore the first CMH statistic. Because the SCORES= option is not specified in this example, PROC FREQ uses the default table scores to calculate the Row Mean Scores Differ statistic, which has a value of 7.963 and a p-value of .047. This statistic has $4 - 1 = 3$ degrees of freedom because the row variable has four levels. At an alpha level of .05, you can conclude from this result that, for at least one stratum, the means of the column values (age groups) are not the same for all rows of the table. In other words, the important factors involved in choosing a car depend upon the age group of the person making the choice.

The test of general association has a value of 12.384 with a p-value of .415. This statistic has $(4 - 1) * (5 - 1) = 12$ degrees of freedom. From this result, you can conclude that there is no general association between the row variable and the column variable for any stratum. An alternative interpretation of this result is that some pattern of association exists between the row variable and the column variable, but it lacks sufficient strength or consistency to dominate any other pattern.

In addition to examining the summary statistics, you should also closely examine the statistics for the individual strata to determine the nature of the association between the variables.

---

[*]Computing all three CMH statistics can require large amounts of computer memory. To save computer memory, you can specify CMH1 to compute only the first CMH statistic or CMH2 to compute only the first and second CMH statistics.

Stratified Analysis for 2 × 2 Tables

For 2 × 2 tables, you can use *adjusted relative risk estimates* or *adjusted odds ratios* to measure the average extent of association across strata. As with single (nonstratified) 2 × 2 tables, PROC FREQ computes odds ratios for case-control (retrospective) studies and relative risk for cohort (prospective) studies.

PROC FREQ computes two types of adjusted relative risk estimates:

Mantel-Haenszel estimator with a test-based confidence interval
handles zero frequencies with no difficulty but produces less precise confidence intervals.

Logit estimator with a precision-based confidence interval
adds 0.5 to each cell of any table that contains a zero frequency because cells with frequency counts of zero pose a computational problem for this estimator.

PROC FREQ also computes another relevant statistic only for the stratified analysis of 2 × 2 tables. The Breslow-Day statistic tests the null hypothesis that the odds ratios from the q strata are all equal. That is, it tests the homogeneity of the odds ratios across strata. If the Breslow-Day statistic is significant, then there is some type of interaction among the row variable, the column variable, and the stratification variables. Note, however, that homogeneity of odds ratios has no bearing on the validity of the adjusted relative risk estimates. The Breslow-Day statistic is a chi-square test with $q - 1$ degrees of freedom and is valid only if you have a large sample size in each stratum. That is, you need at least a sample size of approximately 20 in each stratum.

Recall the CARSALES data used previously for the example in "Tests of No Association for a Single 2 × 2 Table." Those data showed the relationship between customers' receiving a rebate coupon and their purchasing a car from your dealership. Instead of having data for only one dealership, suppose you now have similar data, in a data set called CARSAL3, from three different dealerships in different states.

The following example produces the crosstabulation tables and computes the adjusted relative risk estimates for the CARSAL3 data. Use the CMH option in the TABLES statement to compute the statistics for the stratified analysis. Output 5.10 shows the results.

```
proc freq data=carsal3 order=data;
   tables dealer*coupon*purchase / nopercent
                                   nocol
                                   norow
                                   cmh;
   weight count;
run;
```

Output 5.10
Adjusted Relative
Risk Estimates for
2 × 2 Tables

```
                              Car Survey Data                          1

                      TABLE 1 OF COUPON BY PURCHASE
                         CONTROLLING FOR DEALER=1

          COUPON     PURCHASE

          Frequency|Y       |N       | Total
          ---------+--------+--------+
          Y        |   13 |    47 |     60
          ---------+--------+--------+
          N        |    4 |    56 |     60
          ---------+--------+--------+
          Total        17      103     120


                      TABLE 2 OF COUPON BY PURCHASE
                         CONTROLLING FOR DEALER=2

          COUPON     PURCHASE

          Frequency|Y       |N       | Total
          ---------+--------+--------+
          Y        |    5 |    45 |     50
          ---------+--------+--------+
          N        |    3 |    47 |     50
          ---------+--------+--------+
          Total         8       92     100


                      TABLE 3 OF COUPON BY PURCHASE
                         CONTROLLING FOR DEALER=3

          COUPON     PURCHASE

          Frequency|Y       |N       | Total
          ---------+--------+--------+
          Y        |   15 |    42 |     57
          ---------+--------+--------+
          N        |    9 |    48 |     57
          ---------+--------+--------+
          Total        24       90     114
```

```
                              Car Survey Data                          2

               SUMMARY STATISTICS FOR COUPON BY PURCHASE
                         CONTROLLING FOR DEALER


          Cochran-Mantel-Haenszel Statistics (Based on Table Scores)

          Statistic  Alternative Hypothesis     DF     Value     Prob
          ---------------------------------------------------------------
              1       Nonzero Correlation         1     7.004    0.008
              2       Row Mean Scores Differ      1     7.004    0.008
              3       General Association         1     7.004    0.008
```

```
                 Estimates of the Common Relative Risk (Row1/Row2)
                                                        95%
          Type of Study   Method           Value   Confidence Bounds
          -----------------------------------------------------------------
          Case-Control    Mantel-Haenszel  2.364    1.250    4.470
            (Odds Ratio)  Logit            2.324    1.207    4.473

          Cohort          Mantel-Haenszel  2.063    1.207    3.526
            (Col1 Risk)   Logit            2.001    1.148    3.488

          Cohort          Mantel-Haenszel  0.887    0.812    0.969
            (Col2 Risk)   Logit            0.904    0.833    0.982

          The confidence bounds for the M-H estimates are test-based.



                 Breslow-Day Test for Homogeneity of the Odds Ratios

          Chi-Square =   1.049          DF =   2          Prob = 0.592


          Total Sample Size = 334
```

Interpretation of output

The adjusted relative risk estimates are listed in the table labeled "Estimates of the Common Relative Risk (Row1/Row2)." Note that the Mantel-Haenszel and the Logit estimators are similar. As the sample size increases and the number of zero frequencies decreases, the two estimators become closer and closer. Looking at the adjusted relative risk estimate labeled Cohort (Col1 Risk) you can conclude that customers who receive a rebate coupon are about twice as likely as customers who do not receive a coupon to purchase a car from one of the three dealerships.

Regardless of how the data are collected (prospectively or retrospectively), the adjusted odds ratios are of interest in stratified analysis of 2 × 2 tables. In this example, the statistic labeled Case-Control (Odds Ratio) has a value of about 2.3, which is similar to the value of 2.0 for the adjusted relative risk.

The Breslow-Day Test, listed at the bottom of Output 5.10, tests the homogeneity of the odds ratios among all strata. The value of this statistic is 1.049 with a p-value of .592. You can conclude that the odds ratios are homogeneous across the three strata (dealerships). That is, coupons have approximately the same effect on customers at all three dealerships.

Tests of No Association for Matched Pairs

When you have matched pairs sampled from a single population, such as husbands and wives, or repeated measurements on the same people at two different time periods, you cannot use the regular Pearson chi-square to test for no association between the row variable and the column variable. The Pearson chi-square test assumes that the row and column variables are independent, but matched pairs are not independent. If the response variable has two levels, then you can use McNemar's test, which is a special case of a CMH statistic, to test for no association.

Suppose you have taken a survey of potential car buyers before and after an advertising campaign aimed at increasing sales of cars. You ask the people before the campaign if they would seriously consider buying a car from your dealership. The response can be either 'Y' (yes) or 'N' (no). Then, after the advertising campaign is completed, you ask the same people again if they would seriously consider buying a car from your dealership. The following statements enter the survey data into a SAS data set called ADSALES and use PROC FREQ to create the crosstabulation table shown in Output 5.11:

```
data adsales;
   input pre $ post $ count;
   cards;
Y Y 8
Y N 1
N Y 5
N N 17
;

proc freq data=adsales order=data;
   tables pre*post / nopercent nocol norow;
   weight count;
run;
```

Output 5.11
Crosstabulation
Table for Matched
Pairs

```
                      Car Survey Data

                   TABLE OF PRE BY POST

        PRE       POST

        Frequency|Y        |N        | Total
        ---------+---------+---------+
        Y        |    8 |      1 |     9
        ---------+---------+---------+
        N        |    5 |     17 |    22
        ---------+---------+---------+
        Total         13        18       31
```

You can see from the table in Output 5.11 that six people's opinions were affected by the advertising campaign. One person changed their answer from 'Y' to 'N', and five people changed their answer from 'N' to 'Y'. These are the only cells of the table necessary to compute McNemar's test. The general form of McNemar's test is shown in the following equation, where $n12$ and $n21$ are the upper right and lower left cells, respectively, of the two-by-two table:

$$Q_M = (n12 - n21)^2 / (n12 + n21) \quad .$$

Note that McNemar's test has one degree of freedom.

For the data shown in Output 5.11, McNemar's test for no association is calculated as follows:

$$Q_M = (1 - 5)^2 / (1 + 5) = 2.667 \quad .$$

You can compute the McNemar's test statistic and its associated probability value directly in a DATA step. This example uses the PROBCHI function to calculate a significance test for the statistic. PROC PRINT lists the data set containing the McNemar's test statistic, its degrees of freedom, and its probability value in Output 5.12.

```
data mcnemar;
   df=1;                        /* assign 1 degree of freedom  */
   stat=(5-1)**2/(5+1);         /* compute the test statistic  */
   prob=1-probchi(stat,df);     /* compute the probability value */
run;

proc print data=mcnemar;
run;
```

Output 5.12
McNemar's Test for
Matched Pairs

```
                           Car Survey Data

                OBS    DF     STAT      PROB

                 1     1    2.66667   0.10247
```

Interpretation of output

You compute a value of 2.667 for McNemar's test with a probability value of .102. You can conclude (at the .05 alpha level) that there is no association between persons' considering buying a car from your dealership before the advertising campaign and their considering buying a car from your dealership after the campaign. In other words, the advertising campaign had no statistically significant effect on people.

Learning More

□ For complete reference information on PROC FREQ, see the *SAS Procedures Guide, Version 6, Third Edition*, or the *SAS/STAT User's Guide, Version 6, Fourth Edition, Volume 1 and Volume 2*.

□ For more information on using the FORMAT procedure to create formats, see the *SAS Procedures Guide, Version 6, Third Edition*.

References

□ Breslow, N. (1982), "Covariance Adjustment of Relative-Risk Estimates in Matched Studies," *Biometrics*, 38, 661-672.

□ Breslow, N.E. and Day, N.E. (1980), *Statistical Methods in Cancer Research, Volume 1: The Analysis of Case-Control Studies*, Lyon: International Agency for Research on Cancer.

□ Fleiss, J. L. (1981), *Statistical Methods for Rates and Proportions*, Second Edition, New York: John Wiley & Sons Inc.

□ Hays, W.L. (1981), *Statistics*, Third Edition, New York: Holt, Rinehart, and Winston, Inc.

□ Kleinbaum, D.G., Kupper, L.L., Morganstern, H. (1982), *Epidemiological Research: Principles and Quantitative Methods*, Belmont, CA: Wadsworth, Inc.

□ Mantel, N. (1963), "Chi-square Tests with One Degree of Freedom: Extensions of the Mantel-Haenszel Procedure," *Journal of the American Statistical Association*, 58, 690-700.

□ Mantel, N. and Haenszel, W. (1959), "Statistical Aspects of the Analysis of Data from Retrospective Studies of Disease," *Journal of the National Cancer Institute*, 22, 719-748.

Chapter 6 Analyzing Quantitative Marketing Data

Introduction

You can analyze quantitative marketing data using SAS software. Quantitative variables typically have a relatively large number of different levels, and these levels always have at least some inherent order. You measure quantitative data with an ordinal, interval, or ratio scale of measurement, but never with a nominal scale. In contrast, qualitative data typically fall into a small number of categories. You usually measure qualitative data on a nominal scale although you can treat data measured on any scale as qualitative if the number of distinct levels is small. Most of the analyses you perform on quantitative data are invalid or irrelevant for qualitative data. For more information on the distinction between qualitative and quantitative data and information on measurement levels, see Chapter 1, "Introduction."

Quantitative variables consist of numeric values. You can calculate statistics such as means and variances for individual variables, and you can perform significance tests for relevant hypotheses involving one or more variables. In this chapter, you see how to produce tests of correlation and association for quantitative marketing data. You also learn how to use SAS software to perform tests of means and proportions, and you learn various types of regression analysis.

Chapter 5, "Analyzing Qualitative Marketing Data," explains how to produce tables, compute measures of association, and perform tests of no association for marketing data that can be classified as qualitative.

SAS Data Example

The data used for most of the examples in this chapter concern factors considered to be influential in determining the cost of providing air service. The source of the data is a Civil Aeronautics Board report, "Aircraft Operations Costs and Performance Report," August, 1972. The variables in the AIRLINE data set are

CPM	cost per passenger mile (in cents)
ALF	average load factor (% of seats occupied by passengers)
ASL	average length of nonstop legs of flights (1000 miles)
SPA	average number of seats per aircraft (100 seats)
UTL	average hours per day use of aircraft.

Data have been collected for a sample of thirty-three US airlines with average nonstop lengths of flights greater than 800 miles. The DATA step to input these data appears in the appendix. The following code lists the AIRLINE data set, as shown in Output 6.1:

```
proc print data=airline;
   title 'Airline Cost Data';
run;
```

Output 6.1
Listing of Airline Cost Data

```
                          Airline Cost Data

          OBS    CPM     ALF     ASL      SPA      UTL

            1   3.306   0.287   1.528   0.3522    8.09
            2   3.527   0.349   2.189   0.3279    9.56
            3   3.959   0.362   1.518   0.1356   10.80
            4   4.737   0.378   0.821   0.1290    5.65
            5   3.096   0.381   1.692   0.3007   10.20
            6   3.689   0.394   0.949   0.1488    7.94
            7   2.357   0.397   3.607   0.3390   13.30
            8   2.833   0.400   1.495   0.3597    8.42
            9   3.313   0.405   0.863   0.1390    9.57
           10   3.044   0.409   0.845   0.1390    9.00
           11   2.846   0.410   0.840   0.1390    9.62
           12   2.341   0.412   1.350   0.1920    7.91
           13   2.780   0.417   2.377   0.3287    8.83
           14   3.392   0.422   1.031   0.1365    8.35
           15   3.856   0.425   2.780   0.1282   10.60
           16   3.462   0.426   0.975   0.2025    7.52
           17   2.711   0.434   1.912   0.3148    8.36
           18   2.743   0.439   1.584   0.1607    8.43
           19   3.760   0.452   1.164   0.1270    7.55
           20   3.311   0.455   1.236   0.1221    7.70
           21   2.404   0.466   1.123   0.1481    9.38
           22   2.962   0.476   0.961   0.1236    8.91
           23   3.437   0.476   1.416   0.1145    7.27
           24   2.906   0.478   1.392   0.1148    8.71
           25   3.140   0.486   0.877   0.1060    8.29
           26   2.275   0.488   2.515   0.3546    9.50
           27   2.954   0.495   0.871   0.1186    8.44
           28   3.306   0.504   1.408   0.1345    9.47
           29   2.425   0.535   1.576   0.1361   10.80
           30   2.971   0.539   1.008   0.1150    6.84
           31   4.024   0.541   0.823   0.0943    6.31
           32   2.363   0.582   1.963   0.1381    8.48
           33   2.258   0.591   1.790   0.1375    7.87
```

Basic Tests and Measures for Quantitative Marketing Data

A first step in data analysis is to examine the sample data. You can compute several different tests and measures for your data to give you an idea about trends and patterns in your data, the presence of unusual values, the distribution of your data, and how closely different variables in your data are related to each other. Basic tests and measures of data include descriptive statistics, tests of normality, plots of data, and measures of association and correlation.

Computing Descriptive Statistics

Descriptive statistics provide useful information about your sample data, such as measures of central tendency, measures of variability, and other characteristics of the data distribution. You often want to examine descriptive statistics, such as the mean, median, and variance of your data sample to see if these values are within expected ranges. Extreme or unusual values may indicate the presence of outliers, data entry errors, or other problems with your data. You can use the UNIVARIATE procedure to compute all of the different measures described in this section.

Measures of Central Tendency

□ The population *mean*, μ, is usually estimated by the sample mean:

$$\bar{x} = \Sigma x_i / n \quad .$$

□ The population *median* is the central value, lying above and below half of the population values. The sample median is the middle value when the data are arranged in ascending or descending order. For an even number of observations, the midpoint between the two middle values is usually reported as the median.

□ The *mode* is the value at which the density of the population is at a maximum. The sample mode is the value that occurs most often in the sample.

Quantiles

Quantiles, including percentiles, quartiles, and the median, are useful for examining a distribution. For a set of measurements arranged in order of magnitude, the pth percentile is the value that has $p\%$ of the measurements below it and $(100-p)\%$ above it. The median is the 50th percentile. The upper quartile is the 75th percentile and the lower quartile is the 25th percentile.

Measures of Variability

□ The *range* is the difference between the largest and the smallest values in the sample.

□ The *interquartile range* is the difference between the upper and lower quartiles.

□ The population *variance*, usually denoted by σ^2, is the expected value of the squared difference of the values from the population mean. The sample variance, denoted s^2, is usually computed as

$$s^2 = \Sigma \left(x_i - \bar{x} \right)^2 / (n - 1) \quad .$$

□ The *standard deviation* is the square root of the variance. The standard deviation is expressed in the same units as the observations, rather than in squared units.

Using the UNIVARIATE Procedure

Use the sample statements shown below to compute descriptive statistics for the airline cost data using PROC UNIVARIATE. Output 6.2 shows the results for the CPM variable only. PROC UNIVARIATE produces similar output for each numeric variable in the input data set.

```
proc univariate data=airline;
run;
```

Output 6.2
Computing
Descriptive
Statistics with
PROC
UNIVARIATE

```
                          Airline Cost Data

                        Univariate Procedure

     Variable=CPM          Cost per mile

        ❶   Moments

                 N              33   Sum Wgts          33
                 Mean     3.105697   Sum          102.488
                 Std Dev  0.584398   Variance     0.341521
                 Skewness 0.588852   Kurtosis     0.410186
                 USS      329.2253   CSS          10.92867
                 CV       18.81697   Std Mean     0.101731
                 T:Mean=0 30.52863   Pr>|T|         0.0001
                 Num ^= 0       33   Num > 0           33
                 M(Sign)      16.5   Pr>=|M|        0.0001
                 Sgn Rank    280.5   Pr>=|S|        0.0001


        ❷   Quantiles(Def=5)

                 100% Max    4.737      99%    4.737
                  75% Q3     3.437      95%    4.024
                  50% Med    3.044      90%    3.856
                  25% Q1     2.743      10%    2.357
                   0% Min    2.258       5%    2.275
                                         1%    2.258

                 Range       2.479
                 Q3-Q1       0.694
                 Mode        3.306


        ❸   Extremes

                 Lowest   Obs    Highest   Obs
                 2.258(    33)     3.76(    19)
                 2.275(    26)    3.856(    15)
                 2.341(    12)    3.959(     3)
                 2.357(     7)    4.024(    31)
                 2.363(    32)    4.737(     4)
```

Interpretation of output

The circled numbers in the output correspond to the numbers in the following list:

❶ Under Moments, PROC UNIVARIATE lists several descriptive statistics including the mean, variance, and standard deviation.

❷ Under Quantiles, PROC UNIVARIATE lists the median, mode, range, and interquartile range (labeled Q3-Q1), along with several percentile values.

❸ Under Extremes, PROC UNIVARIATE lists the five lowest and the five highest values for the CPM variable.

For complete reference information on PROC UNIVARIATE, see the *SAS Procedures Guide*.

Testing for Normality

You can test if your data are distributed normally so that you can test hypotheses based on an assumption of normally distributed data.

You can use PROC UNIVARIATE to test the null hypothesis that your data are a random sample from a normal distribution. Many statistical tests are valid only for data that come from a normal distribution. Specify the NORMAL option in the PROC UNIVARIATE statement to request that PROC UNIVARIATE compute one of two tests of normality.

If the sample size is less than or equal to 2,000, then PROC UNIVARIATE computes the Shapiro-Wilk statistic, W. The test statistic is labeled W:NORMAL and its p-value is labeled PROB<W in the output. If the sample size is greater than 2,000, then PROC UNIVARIATE computes the Kolmogorov D statistic. This test statistic is labeled D:NORMAL, and its p-value is labeled PROB>D in the output. If the probability value is less than your chosen significance level (such as .05), you can reject the null hypothesis and conclude that the data do not come from a normal distribution. The test for normality is listed at the bottom of the section of the output labeled Moments.

The following sample statements use PROC UNIVARIATE to test the normality of the airline cost data. Output 6.3 shows only a portion of the full PROC UNIVARIATE output produced by this program.

```
proc univariate data=airline normal;
run;
```

Output 6.3
Testing Data for
Normality with
PROC
UNIVARIATE
(Partial Output)

```
                          Airline Cost Data

                        Univariate Procedure

    Variable=CPM          Cost per mile

                              Moments

              N                33   Sum Wgts         33
              Mean        3.105697   Sum         102.488
              Std Dev     0.584398   Variance   0.341521
              Skewness    0.588852   Kurtosis   0.410186
              USS         329.2253   CSS        10.92867
              CV          18.81697   Std Mean   0.101731
              T:Mean=0    30.52863   Pr>|T|       0.0001
              Num ^= 0          33   Num > 0          33
              M(Sign)         16.5   Pr>=|M|      0.0001
              Sgn Rank       280.5   Pr>=|S|      0.0001
              W:Normal     0.95562   Pr<W         0.2384
```

Interpretation of output

The test for normality appears at the bottom of the Moments section in the PROC UNIVARIATE output. Output 6.3 shows the Moments section for the CPM variable with the test for normality highlighted at the bottom. The values of the test for normality for all the variables in the airline cost data are displayed in Table 6.1.

Table 6.1
Tests of Normality
for Airline Cost
Data

Variable	Test Statistic	Probability Value
CPM	0.95562	0.2384
ALF	0.978806	0.7966
ASL	0.858964	0.0004
SPA	0.727419	0.0001
UTL	0.958376	0.2833

You can see that the ASL and SPA variables have small p-values for the Shapiro-Wilk test of normality. The other three variables have p-values above the .05 level of significance. Thus, you can use the CPM, ALF, and UTL variables in statistical analyses that require normally distributed data.

Plotting Data

Plot your data to examine relationships between pairs of variables or to look for trends and patterns in your data. Plots can give you rough measure of the strength of association between variables. Some of the methods discussed in Chapter 4, "Producing Marketing Reports," may also be relevant to your examining raw data.

Use the PLOT procedure to plot your raw data in a line-printer quality graph. The PS= option in the OPTIONS statement requests that only 30 lines be printed per page. The following example shows how to plot the CPM variable against the ALF variable from the AIRLINE data set, as shown in Output 6.4:

```
options ps=30;
proc plot data=airline;
   plot cpm*alf;
run;
```

Output 6.4
Plotting Airline Cost Data with PROC PLOT

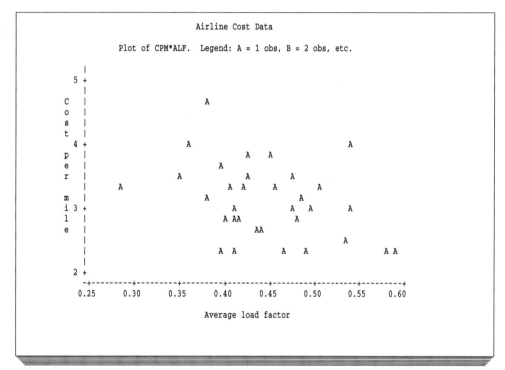

For high-resolution graphics, use the GPLOT procedure from SAS/GRAPH software to plot data. In the following program, use the VALUE= option in the SYMBOL1 statement to assign a value to the plotting symbol in the graph. In this example, the symbols are plotted with a star, instead of the default, which is a plus sign (+). The resulting plot is shown in Output 6.5.

```
proc gplot data=airline;
   symbol1 value=star;
   plot cpm*alf;
run;
```

Output 6.5
Plotting Airline Cost
Data with PROC
GPLOT

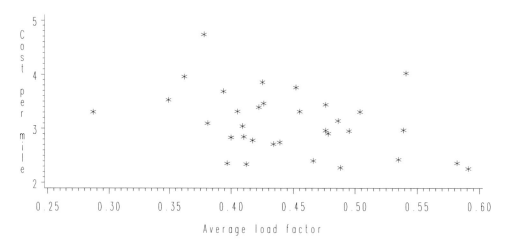

In Output 6.4 and Output 6.5, you can see the general tendency that higher values for average load factor (ALF) are associated with lower values for costs per mile (CPM). However, the association is not very strong.

See the section, "Plotting the Regression Line," later in this chapter for an example of the same scatter plot with a regression line added to the plot.

Measuring Correlation

If you have two or more related variables, you may want to examine the correlation between the variables. Correlation measures the degree of association between two or more quantitative variables. The most common measure of correlation between two or more variables is the Pearson correlation coefficient, also called the Pearson product-moment correlation. You can use PROC CORR to compute the Pearson correlation coefficient. PROC CORR also computes other measures of association for quantitative variables:

□ Spearman's rank-order correlation coefficient is a nonparametric measure calculated from the ranks of the data.

□ Kendall's tau-b is a measure of association calculated from concordances and discordances for paired observations.

□ Hoeffding's measure of dependence, D, is another measure of association that is more sensitive to general departures from independence than are the correlation measures.

The following sample statements show how to use PROC CORR to compute the Pearson correlation coefficients for all the variables in the AIRLINE data set. The results are shown in Output 6.6.

```
proc corr data=airline;
run;
```

Output 6.6
Computing Pearson
Correlation
Coefficients with
PROC CORR

```
                           Airline Cost Data                        1

                          Correlation Analysis

           5 'VAR' Variables:  CPM     ALF     ASL     SPA     UTL


                           Simple Statistics
                         ❶          ❷          ❸                ❺
            Variable     N         Mean       Std Dev          Sum

            CPM          33      3.105697    0.584398      102.488000
            ALF          33      0.445788    0.066931       14.711000
            ASL          33      1.469061    0.649978       48.479000
            SPA          33      0.183579    0.089700        6.058100
            UTL          33      8.717273    1.449026      287.670000

                           Simple Statistics
                         ❻          ❼
            Variable   Minimum    Maximum   Label

            CPM        2.258000   4.737000  Cost per mile
            ALF        0.287000   0.591000  Average load factor
            ASL        0.821000   3.607000  Average flight length
            SPA        0.094300   0.359700  Average seats per aircraft
            UTL        5.650000  13.300000  Average hours per day use of aircraft
```

```
                           Airline Cost Data                        2

                          Correlation Analysis

     Pearson Correlation Coefficients / Prob > |R| under Ho: Rho=0 / N = 33

                                           CPM        ALF        ASL

     CPM                                 1.00000   -0.37378   -0.35078
     Cost per mile                         0.0      0.0321     0.0453

     ALF                                -0.37378    1.00000   -0.08719
     Average load factor                  0.0321     0.0        0.6295

     ASL                                -0.35078   -0.08719    1.00000
     Average flight length                0.0453     0.6295     0.0

     SPA                                -0.29758   -0.49490    0.60710
     Average seats per aircraft           0.0926     0.0034     0.0002

     UTL                                -0.37197   -0.20538    0.62842
     Average hours per day use of aircraft 0.0330    0.2515     0.0001

                                           SPA        UTL

     CPM                                -0.29758   -0.37197
     Cost per mile                        0.0926     0.0330

     ALF                                -0.49490   -0.20538
     Average load factor                  0.0034     0.2515

     ASL                                 0.60710    0.62842
     Average flight length                0.0002     0.0001

     SPA                                 1.00000    0.32442
     Average seats per aircraft           0.0        0.0655

     UTL                                 0.32442    1.00000
     Average hours per day use of aircraft 0.0655     0.0
```

Interpretation of output

For each variable, PROC CORR prints descriptive statistics at the top of the output. The circled numbers in the output correspond to the numbers in the following list:

❶   the number of nonmissing values

❷   the mean

❸   the standard deviation

❹   (not shown) the median (if you specify the SPEARMAN, KENDALL, or HOEFFDING options)

❺   the sum (if only Pearson correlations are computed)

❻   the minimum value

❼   the maximum value.

You can suppress the printing of these statistics by specifying the NOSIMPLE option in the PROC CORR statement.

For each pair of variables, PROC CORR prints, in a two-way table, the Pearson correlation coefficients and the significance probability of the correlation under the null hypothesis that the statistic is zero.

For the airline cost data, you can see in Output 6.6 that the CPM variable is moderately negatively correlated with the four other variables in the data. The correlation between CPM and ALF is -0.37, which coincides with the negative slope evident in the plots of these variables shown previously in Output 6.4 and Output 6.5. Note, however, that the correlation of -0.29758 between CPM and SPA is not significantly different from 0 (at the 0.05 alpha level).

Note: When you simultaneously evaluate numerous inferential statistical tests using an individual alpha value of .05, the probability of incorrectly declaring at least one of the tests significant is higher than .05. The greater the number of tests, the higher the probability of making such an error. A common way of handling this issue is to adjust the alpha value. For more information, see Miller (1981).

Performing Tests of Means

If you have data from two independent samples, you can perform a two-sample, independent-groups *t*-test on the data to test whether the means of the two groups are equal. If you have data from a matched sample, such as married couples, brothers and sisters, or repeated measurements on the same people, you cannot use a two-sample *t*-test to test whether the means of the two groups are equal. Instead, you can test whether the difference between the two matched measurements is significantly different from zero. This is called a *matched-group* or *paired-comparisons t*-test.

Suppose that you have measurements of customer satisfaction (on a scale from 0 to 100) with a sample of your product. You have taken measurements from 10 men and 10 women at two separate times. The first measurement is taken before the presentation of an advertising campaign, and the second measurement is taken after the campaign. You have two experimental questions:

1.   Is there a difference in customer satisfaction between males and females?

2.   Did the advertising campaign affect customer satisfaction?

You can use a two-sample *t*-test to help answer the first question, and a matched-group *t*-test to help answer the second question.

Use the following DATA step to enter the data for this example into a SAS data set called ADTEST. The variables are described in the following list:

ID	contains an identification value for each person in the sample.
GENDER	contains character values describing whether the person is male (M) or female (F).
SCALE1	contains the values of the first measurement of the satisfaction scale.
SCALE2	contains the values of the second measurement of the satisfaction scale.

```
data adtest;
   input id $ gender $ scale1 scale2 @@;
   cards;
101 F 77 92  102 F 63 60  103 M 91 91  104 M 54 47  105 F 85 84
106 M 57 79  107 F 83 89  108 F 38 42  109 F 49 45  110 M 25 28
111 M 90 99  112 M 58 68  113 F 72 70  114 F 80 93  115 M 13 50
116 F 21 39  117 M 60 51  118 F 63 60  119 M 46 70  120 M 77 75
;
```

Tests for Independent Samples

For the customer satisfaction data used in this example, men and women are treated as separate, independent groups. You can perform a two-sample *t*-test to test the hypothesis that the means of the two groups are equal. However, you cannot use both measurements for each person in the sample because the repeated measurements are not independent of each other.

The statements described in the following list show how to use the TTEST procedure to test whether males and females have different mean levels of satisfaction after the presentation of the advertising campaign. Recall that the SCALE2 variable contains the satisfaction scale measurements taken after the advertising campaign.

PROC TTEST statement
   invokes the procedure and enables you to specify the input data set with the DATA= option.

CLASS statement
   identifies the grouping variable from the input data set. The grouping variable must have two, and only two, levels.

VAR statement
   identifies the variables from the input data set whose means are to be compared. If the VAR statement is omitted, all numeric variables in the input data set (unless a numeric variable appears in the CLASS statement) are included in the analysis.

The following program produces the results shown in Output 6.7:

```
proc ttest data=adtest;
   class gender;
   var scale2;
   title 'Customer Satisfaction Data';
run;
```

Output 6.7
Comparing Group
Means with PROC
TTEST

```
                        Customer Satisfaction Data

                           TTEST PROCEDURE

   Variable: SCALE2

   GENDER     N            Mean          Std Dev        Std Error


   ---------------------------------------------------------------
   F         10      67.40000000      21.27178622      6.72672943
   M         10      65.80000000      21.78072542      6.88767014

   Variances       T     DF    Prob>|T|


   ------------------------------------
   Unequal     0.1662   18.0    0.8699
   Equal       0.1662   18.0    0.8699

   For H0: Variances are equal, F' = 1.05    DF = (9,9)   Prob>F' = 0.9450
```

Interpretation of output

For each group, PROC TTEST prints the following descriptive statistics:

□   N, the number of nonmissing values

□   Mean

□   Std Dev, the standard deviation

□   Std Error, the standard error of the mean

□   Minimum value, if the line size allows

□   Maximum value, if the line size allows.

For the assumptions of equal and unequal variances for the two groups, PROC TTEST prints the following:

□   T, the *t* statistic for testing the null hypothesis that the two groups are equal.

□   DF, the degrees of freedom.

□   Prob>|T|, the probability of a greater absolute value of *t* under the null hypothesis. This is the two-tailed significance probability.

At the bottom of the output, PROC TTEST provides an F statistic for testing whether or not the variances of the two groups are equal.

For these data, because the p-value of the F statistic is nonsignificant, you can assume that the variances of the two groups are equal. Females have a mean satisfaction scale value of 67.4, and males have a satisfaction scale value of 65.8. The *t* statistic for testing whether or not the two groups are different is 0.1662, with a p-value of 0.8699. You can conclude that males and females are not significantly different on this scale of satisfaction.

Tests for Matched Samples

The example in this section uses the customer satisfaction data to perform a *t*-test for matched samples. The statements described in this section show how to use the DATA step and the MEANS procedure to test whether the mean change in satisfaction due to the advertising campaign is significantly different from zero.

First, use the DATA step to create a new variable, DIFF, made by subtracting SCALE1 from SCALE2:

```
data adtest2;
   set adtest;
   diff=scale2-scale1;
run;
```

Next, use the PROC MEANS step described in the following list to test whether the DIFF variable is significantly different from zero. For this example, males and females are treated as one homogeneous group.

PROC MEANS statement

invokes the procedure and enables you to specify statistic keywords, which compute and print the requested statistic in the output. For this example, specify the following keywords:

N	the number of nonmissing values
MEAN	the mean, or average
STDERR	the standard error of the mean
T	Student's *t* for testing the hypothesis that the population mean is 0
PRT	the probability of a greater absolute value for the *t*-value above.

VAR statement

specifies the variables for which you want to compute and print statistics.

The following program produces the results shown in Output 6.8:

```
proc means data=adtest2 n mean stderr t prt;
   var diff;
   title 'Customer Satisfaction Data';
run;
```

Output 6.8
Testing Matched Samples with PROC MEANS

```
                        Customer Satisfaction Data

            Analysis Variable : DIFF


            N        Mean      Std Error        T   Prob>|T|
            ------------------------------------------------------
            20    6.5000000    2.6739484    2.4308622    0.0251
            ------------------------------------------------------
```

Interpretation of output

For the customer satisfaction data used in this example, the mean of the DIFF variable is 6.5, with a standard error of 2.67. The *t* statistic testing whether or not this mean is significantly different from zero is 2.43, with a p-value of 0.0251. Using an alpha level of 0.05, you can conclude that the advertising campaign had a significant effect on customer satisfaction, raising it by 6.5 scale points.

Performing Regression Analysis

Regression analysis attempts to model the behavior of a response variable, *y*, as a function of one or more explanatory variables, $x_1, x_2, \ldots, x_m$. The relationship between the response variable and the explanatory variables is expressed formally in a *regression model*. The model attempts to explain the variability in the response variable. The variability in the response variable has two components: a systematic part and a random part. The systematic variation in the response variable can be modeled by the explanatory variables. The random variation in the response variable is the remaining variation that cannot be explained by the model.

You use different types of regression models for different purposes. The following regression models are described in this chapter:

□   Simple linear regression models use a single explanatory variable to explain the behavior of the response variable.

□   Multiple linear regression models use two or more explanatory variables to explain the behavior of the response variable.

□   Logistic regression models explain the behavior of a binary or ordinal-level response variable.

□   Autoregressive models adjust time series data for which the random errors are not independent of each other.

Other types of regression models include multivariate, nonlinear, polynomial, and ridge regression models. For more information on using SAS software to perform regression analysis, see *SAS System for Regression*, the *SAS/STAT User's Guide*, and the *SAS/ETS User's Guide*.

Simple Linear Regression

A simple linear regression model has one explanatory variable to explain the behavior of the response variable, as shown in the following equation:

$$y = \beta_0 + \beta_1 x + \epsilon$$

where

y is the response variable.

β_0 and β_1 are unknown parameters.

x is the explanatory variable, also called the independent or regressor variable.

ϵ is a random error term.

Most linear regression models use the *least squares* method to estimate the regression parameters. This method finds estimates of the parameters that minimize the sum of the squared differences between the actual response variable values and the values of the response variable predicted by the regression equation.

You can use the REG procedure in SAS/STAT software for most types of linear regression analysis. SAS statements described in the following list show how to use PROC REG to perform linear regression analysis with one explanatory variable for the airline cost data:

PROC REG statement
> invokes the procedure and enables you to specify the input data set with the DATA= option.

MODEL statement
> specifies the response variable and the explanatory variable for the regression analysis. You specify the response variable to the left of the equals sign and specify the explanatory variable to the right of the equals sign.

The results are shown in Output 6.9.

```
proc reg data=airline;
   model cpm=alf;
   title 'Airline Cost Data';
run;
```

Output 6.9
Simple Linear
Regression Analysis

```
                             Airline Cost Data

       Model: MODEL1
       Dependent Variable: CPM        Cost per mile

                            Analysis of Variance

                            Sum of         Mean       ❶
           Source      DF   Squares       Square    F Value    Prob>F

           Model        1   1.52682      1.52682     5.034     0.0321
           Error       31   9.40185      0.30329
           C Total     32  10.92867
                                             ❷
              Root MSE      0.55071    R-square     0.1397
              Dep Mean      3.10570    Adj R-sq     0.1120
              C.V.         17.73237
```

```
                        Parameter Estimates
                    ❸
                    Parameter      Standard    T for H0:
        Variable  DF   Estimate        Error  Parameter=0   Prob > |T|

        INTERCEP   1    4.560547   0.65545893       6.958       0.0001
        ALF        1   -3.263548   1.45452657      -2.244       0.0321

                        Variable
        Variable  DF    Label

        INTERCEP   1  Intercept
        ALF        1  Average load factor
```

Interpretation of output

The circled numbers in the output correspond to the numbers in the following list:

❶ The F-value for this model is 5.034 with a p-value of 0.0321. You can conclude that there is a statistically significant relationship between the CPM and ALF variables.

❷ The R-square value is 0.1397, indicating that about 14% of the variability in the CPM variable is explained by the ALF variable.

❸ The parameter estimate for the intercept, β_0, is 4.56. The parameter estimate for ALF, β_1, is -3.26. Both parameter estimates are statistically significant at the 0.05 alpha level.

The regression equation can be written as:

$$\hat{CPM} = 4.56 - 3.26(ALF)$$

where the hat, or caret, (^) over CPM indicates that it is an estimated value.

For more complete information about PROC REG output, see the *SAS/STAT User's Guide* or *SAS System for Regression*.

Note that PROC REG is an interactive procedure, which enables you to issue additional MODEL statements without re-invoking the procedure. PROC REG continues to run until you issue a QUIT statement or invoke another PROC step or a DATA step.

Plotting the Regression Line

PROC GPLOT provides you with an option to overlay the regression line on a scatter plot of data. Specify I=R in the SYMBOL1 statement in PROC GPLOT to fit a linear regression line to the data in the scatter plot. PROC GPLOT uses the PROC REG method to fit the regression line. The first variable specified in the PLOT statement is the response variable, and the second variable specified in the PLOT statement is the explanatory variable.

The following sample statements create a high-resolution graphics scatter plot, as shown previously in Output 6.5, and plot the regression line that shows the relationship between the CPM variable and the ALF variable. The results are shown in Output 6.10.

```
proc gplot data=airline;
   symbol1 value=star i=r;
   plot cpm*alf;
run;
```

Output 6.10
*Plotting the
Regression Line
with PROC GPLOT*

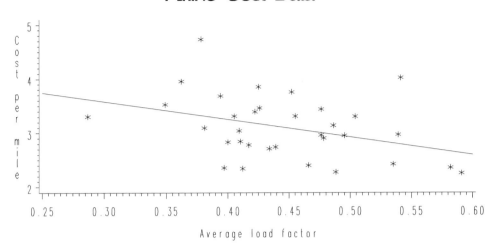

Multiple Linear Regression

The regression model for multiple linear regression is an extension of the model for regression with only one explanatory variable. The following formula shows the general form of the multiple linear regression model:

$$y = \beta_0 + \beta_1 x_1 + \beta_2 x_2 + \dots + \beta_m x_m + \epsilon$$

where

y is the response variable.

$\beta_0, \beta_1, \dots, \beta_m$ are unknown parameters.

$x_1, x_2, \dots, x_m$ are the explanatory variables.

ϵ is a random error term.

The following program produces the results shown in Output 6.11.

```
proc reg data=airline;
   model cpm=alf asl spa utl;
run;
```

Output 6.11
*Multiple Linear
Regression Analysis*

```
                              Airline Cost Data

        Model: MODEL1
        Dependent Variable: CPM        Cost per mile

                           Analysis of Variance

                                Sum of        Mean      ❶
               Source      DF   Squares      Square    F Value     Prob>F

               Model        4   6.57115     1.64279    10.556      0.0001
               Error       28   4.35752     0.15563
               C Total     32  10.92867
```

```
           Root MSE        0.39449    R-square     0.6013 ❷
           Dep Mean        3.10570    Adj R-sq     0.5443
           C.V.           12.70228


                         Parameter Estimates


                         Parameter     Standard    T for H0:
           Variable  DF    Estimate        Error   Parameter=0   Prob > |T|
                         ❸
           INTERCEP   1    8.595525   0.90277548      9.521        0.0001
           ALF        1   -7.211373   1.32056295     -5.461        0.0001
           ASL        1    0.332769   0.18133342      1.835        0.0771
           SPA        1   -4.950301   1.21695241     -4.068        0.0004
           UTL        1   -0.212816   0.06508642     -3.270        0.0029

                         Variable
           Variable  DF    Label

           INTERCEP   1   Intercept
           ALF        1   Average load factor
           ASL        1   Average flight length
           SPA        1   Average seats per aircraft
           UTL        1   Average hours per day use of aircraft
```

Interpretation of output

The circled numbers in the output correspond to the numbers in the following list:

❶ For multiple regression, the F statistic tests the null hypothesis that all regression parameters (except the intercept) are equal to 0. That is, it tests the hypothesis that $\beta_1 = \beta_2 = \beta_3 = \beta_4 = 0$. In this example, the F statistic has a value of 10.556, with a p-value of 0.0001. You can conclude that at least one of the regression parameters is not equal to 0.

❷ The R-square value of 0.6013 indicates that the explanatory variables explain about 60% of the variability in the CPM variable. Note that this value is much higher than the R-square value for the regression model using only the ALF variable to explain CPM (see Output 6.9).

❸ Using rounded values for the parameter estimates, you can write the fitted regression equation as follows:

$$\hat{\text{CPM}} = 8.60 - 7.21(\text{ALF}) + .33(\text{ASL}) - 4.95(\text{SPA}) - .21(\text{UTL}) \qquad .$$

Note, however, that the parameter estimate for ASL has a p-value of 0.0771, which is not significant at the 0.05 alpha level.

Logistic Regression

Logistic regression attempts to model the response probability for a binary or ordinal response variable. For example, logistic regression is useful when you want to use quantitative explanatory variables to explain the behavior of variables with Yes/No responses or Sale/No Sale responses.

Suppose that a binary response variable, y, can have only the values of 1 and 2. Then the expected value of y is the probability, p, that $y = 1$. To facilitate modeling this probability, it is transformed by means of the *logit tranformation*, which is $\log(p / (1 - p))$.

For a binary response variable, the general linear logistic model has the following form:

$$logit(p) = log(p / (1 - p)) = \alpha + \beta_1 x_1 + \beta_2 x_2 + \ldots + \beta_m x_m$$

where

p is the response probability for the response variable y, and logit(p) is the logit transformation of p.

α is the unknown intercept parameter.

$\beta_1, \beta_2, \ldots, \beta_m$ are unknown logistic regression parameters.

$x_1, x_2, \ldots, x_m$ are the explanatory variables.

Logistic regression models use the *maximum likelihood* method to estimate model parameters. The maximum likelihood method attempts to find parameter estimates that maximize the probability that the sample data come from the population represented by the model.

You can fit logistic regression models to data with any of the following SAS/STAT procedures: CATMOD, LIFEREG, LOGISTIC, and PROBIT. The example in this section uses PROC LOGISTIC to perform logistic regression.

Recall the customer satisfaction data used previously in the section, "Performing Tests of Means." Now, suppose that you create a new data set by adding a new binary variable to the original data set. This new variable, BUY, is coded as 1 if the respondent intends to purchase your product and coded as 0 if the respondent does not intend to purchase your product. In this example, you model the probability that a respondent intends to purchase your product, using the SCALE2 variable as a predictor. Recall that SCALE2 contains a measure of customer satisfaction with a sample of your product. The new data set, ADTEST2, is listed in Output 6.12.

Output 6.12
Listing of ADTEST2
Data Set

```
                        Customer Satisfaction Data


        OBS    ID    GENDER    SCALE1    SCALE2    BUY

         1    101      F         77        92       1
         2    102      F         63        60       0
         3    103      M         91        91       1
         4    104      M         54        47       1
         5    105      F         85        84       0
         6    106      M         57        79       0
         7    107      F         83        89       1
         8    108      F         38        42       0
         9    109      F         49        45       0
        10    110      M         25        28       0
        11    111      M         90        99       1
        12    112      M         58        68       1
        13    113      F         72        70       1
        14    114      F         80        93       1
        15    115      M         13        50       0
        16    116      F         21        39       0
        17    117      M         60        51       0
        18    118      F         63        60       0
        19    119      M         46        70       1
        20    120      M         77        75       0
```

The statements and options described in the following list show how to use PROC LOGISTIC to fit a logistic regression model to the customer satisfaction data in the SAS data set, ADTEST2:

PROC LOGISTIC statement

invokes the procedure and enables you to specify the input data set with the DATA= option.

The DESCENDING option reverses the sorting order for the levels of the response variable. For these data, it causes PROC LOGISTIC to model the probability that the response variable is equal to 1.

MODEL statement

specifies the form of the logistic regression model. You specify the binary or ordinal-scale response variable to the left of the equals sign and specify the explanatory variable or variables to the right of the equals sign.

OUTPUT statement

creates a new SAS data set that contains all the variables in the input data set and other variables that you can add to the data set by specifying keywords and assigning variable names to them. In this example, specify the following keywords:

PRED	predicted probabilities of the modeled event
LOWER	lower 95% confidence limits for the predicted probabilities
UPPER	upper 95% confidence limits for the predicted probabilities.

The results of the following program are shown in Output 6.13.

```
proc logistic data=adtest2 descending;
   model buy=scale2;
   output out=adtest3 pred=prob lower=l95 upper=u95;
   title 'Customer Satisfaction Data';
run;
```

Output 6.13
Logistic Regression
Analysis

```
                        Customer Satisfaction Data

                          The LOGISTIC Procedure

        Data Set: WORK.ADTEST2
        Response Variable: BUY
        Response Levels: 2
        Number of Observations: 20
        Link Function: Logit

                               ❶
                          Response Profile

                       Ordered
                         Value    BUY     Count

                           1       1        9
                           2       0       11
```

```
                              ❷
                     Criteria for Assessing Model Fit

                                  Intercept
                       Intercept     and
        Criterion        Only      Covariates    Chi-Square for Covariates

        AIC             29.526       23.613          .
        SC              30.521       25.605          .
        -2 LOG L        27.526       19.613          7.912 with 1 DF (p=0.0049)
        Score             .            .            6.918 with 1 DF (p=0.0085)

                    RSquare = 0.3267        Adjusted RSquare = 0.4371


                              ❸
                     Analysis of Maximum Likelihood Estimates

                     Parameter Standard    Wald       Pr >    Standardized   Odds
        Variable DF  Estimate   Error   Chi-Square Chi-Square   Estimate     Ratio

        INTERCPT 1    -5.4614   2.4201    5.0927     0.0240         .         0.004
        SCALE2   1     0.0771   0.0338    5.1994     0.0226     0.890956      1.080
              ❹
          Association of Predicted Probabilities and Observed Responses

                    Concordant = 83.8%        Somers' D = 0.677
                    Discordant = 16.2%        Gamma     = 0.677
                    Tied       =  0.0%        Tau-a     = 0.353
                    (99 pairs)                c         = 0.838
```

Interpretation of output

The PROC LOGISTIC output consists of several sections. The circled numbers on the output correspond to the numbers in the following list:

❶ The Response Profile section lists the number of values for each level of the response variable.

❷ The Criteria for Assessing Model Fit section lists statistics describing how well the model fits the data. Akaike's Information Criterion (AIC), Schwarz's Criterion (SC), and the -2 Log Likelihood statistic can all be used to compare different models for the same data. Lower values of these statistics indicate a better fit of the model to the data. The Score statistic is a Chi-square statistic that tests the joint effect of all explanatory variables in the model. PROC LOGISTIC also prints an R-Square and adjusted R-square statistic.

❸ The Analysis of Maximum Likelihood Estimates section lists the parameter estimates for the model, along with standard errors, Chi-square statistics, probability values for the Chi-square statistics, standardized estimates, and odds ratios. For these data, you can see that the SCALE2 variable has a parameter estimate of 0.0771 with a standard error of 0.0338. This parameter estimate is statistically significant, with a p-value of 0.0226. The positive value of the parameter estimate indicates that the likelihood of purchasing the product increases as the value of SCALE2 increases.

❹ The Association of Predicted Probabilities and Observed Responses section describes how closely the responses predicted by the model match the observed responses from the data. PROC LOGISTIC prints a measure of concordance, expressed as a percentage.

Also printed are Somers' D, Gamma, Tau-a, and c, which are indices of rank correlation. The higher the index value, the better the predictive ability of the model.

For complete reference information on PROC LOGISTIC output, see the *SAS/STAT User's Guide*.

Listing Predicted Probabilities

After the PROC LOGISTIC step, you use the PROC PRINT step to list the OUT= output data set from PROC LOGISTIC containing the predicted response probabilities and 95% confidence limits for the probabilities. Note that you can change the confidence level by specifying a value for the ALPHA= option in the OUTPUT statement of PROC LOGISTIC. For example, specify ALPHA=0.01 to produce 99% confidence limits.

The data set is listed in Output 6.14.

```
proc print data=adtest3;
   title 'Predicted Probabilities and Confidence Limits';
run;
```

Output 6.14
Predicted
Probabilities from
Logistic Regression
Analysis

```
                    Predicted Probabilities and Confidence Limits
                                         ❶        ❷              ❸
     OBS   ID   GENDER  SCALE1  SCALE2  BUY  _LEVEL_    PROB      L95      U95

      1   101    F        77      92     1      1     0.83597  0.44718  0.96980
      2   102    F        63      60     0      1     0.30206  0.10846  0.60624
      3   103    M        91      91     1      1     0.82513  0.44118  0.96575
      4   104    M        54      47     1      1     0.13713  0.02417  0.50487
      5   105    F        85      84     1      1     0.73342  0.39234  0.92140
      6   106    M        57      79     0      1     0.65175  0.34727  0.86813
      7   107    F        83      89     1      1     0.80177  0.42856  0.95616
      8   108    F        38      42     0      1     0.09756  0.01262  0.47768
      9   109    F        49      45     0      1     0.11989  0.01869  0.49348
     10   110    M        25      28     0      1     0.03545  0.00188  0.41730
     11   111    M        90      99     1      1     0.89734  0.48441  0.98785
     12   112    M        58      68     1      1     0.44498  0.21048  0.70684
     13   113    F        72      70     1      1     0.48329  0.23820  0.73669
     14   114    F        80      93     1      1     0.84627  0.45297  0.97340
     15   115    M        13      50     0      1     0.16685  0.03521  0.52352
     16   116    F        21      39     0      1     0.07901  0.00846  0.46314
     17   117    M        60      51     0      1     0.17784  0.03980  0.53023
     18   118    F        63      60     0      1     0.30206  0.10846  0.60624
     19   119    M        46      70     1      1     0.48329  0.23820  0.73669
     20   120    M        77      75     0      1     0.57895  0.30311  0.81297
```

Interpretation of output

The circled numbers on the output correspond to the numbers in the following list:

❶ PROC LOGISTIC also adds the variable _LEVEL_ to the output data set. The predicted probabilities listed in the OUT= output data set represent the probabilities that the response variable is less than or equal to the value of _LEVEL_.

❷ The PROB variable contains the predicted probabilities that the respondent intends to purchase the product.

❸ The L95 and U95 variables contain the lower and upper 95% confidence limits for the probabilities.

Correcting for Autocorrelation

When you analyze time series data, that is, data that have been collected over time, the errors are typically not independent across time. Instead, the errors are *autocorrelated*. If the errors are autocorrelated, then the standard error estimates are biased, and significance tests for regression parameters are invalid. To correct for the presence of autocorrelation in the data, you include autoregressive parameters in your regression model.

For autoregressive models, you can use any of several different methods to estimate parameters, including variations on the least squares method, the maximum likelihood method, and iterative methods.

You can use the Durbin-Watson d statistic to test for autocorrelation (Durbin and Watson 1951). The d statistic is a ratio with a range from 0 to 4. Values near 2 indicate that the data are not autocorrelated. Values significantly less than 2 indicate positive autocorrelation, where errors of one sign tend to be followed by errors of the same sign. Values significantly above 2 indicate negative autocorrelation, where errors of one sign tend to be followed by errors of the opposite sign. Tables for the d statistic are listed in most econometrics textbooks, such as Johnston (1984) or Pindyck and Rubinfeld (1991). You can also obtain a significance test for the d statistic directly in the AUTOREG and PDLREG procedures in SAS/ETS software.

After you determine that a correction for autocorrelation is needed, you select the order of the autoregressive model to use. One way to select the order of the autoregressive model is *stepwise autoregression.* The stepwise autoregressive model initially fits a high-order model with many autoregressive parameters and then sequentially removes autoregressive parameters until all remaining autoregressive parameters have significant t-tests. If you have no reason to expect a specific type of autoregressive model for your data, then you may want to use this method.

Suppose you are interested in analyzing the house construction market in the U.S. You have information on monthly construction contracts (in millions of dollars), average new home mortgage interest rates, and private housing starts (in thousands of units) for the period January 1983 to October 1989. These values are actual data taken from the *Survey of Current Business* (U.S. Department of Commerce 1990).

The following statements read the data into a SAS data set called HOUSECON. The data set consists of the following variables:

DATE   contains the date in a MONYY format.

CONSTR   contains the construction contracts.

INTRATE   contains the new home mortgage interest rate.

HSTARTS   contains the housing starts.

To conserve space, only a portion of the DATA step is shown. The full data set is shown in the appendix.

```
data housecon;
   title 'Construction Data';
   label date='Date'
         constr='Construction contracts (in $1,000,000)'
         intrate='New home mortgage interest rate'
         hstarts='Housing Starts (in 1000s)';
   input date:monyy5. constr intrate hstarts @@;
   format date monyy5.;
   cards;
```

```
JAN83 11358 13.00  91.3 FEB83 11355 12.62  96.3
MAR83 16100 12.97 134.6 APR83 16315 12.02 135.8
MAY83 19205 12.21 174.9 JUN83 20263 11.90 173.2
 more data lines
;
```

You can use PROC AUTOREG to perform the following tasks for these data:

1. Compute the Durbin-Watson *d* statistic to test for the presence of autocorrelation.

2. Calculate the p-value for the *d* statistic.

3. Fit a stepwise autoregressive model to the data to correct for the presence of autocorrelation.

You may want to test for the presence of autocorrelation first, then fit an autoregressive model in a separate step only if you find that the data are, in fact, autocorrelated. For demonstration purposes in this example, however, both tasks are performed in the same PROC AUTOREG step. The following list of statements and options describes the PROC AUTOREG step used in this example:

PROC AUTOREG statement
>   invokes the procedure and enables you to use the DATA= option to specify the name of the input data set containing the analysis variables.

MODEL statement
>   specifies the form of the regression model. In this example, HSTARTS is the dependent variable, and CONSTR and INTRATE are the independent explanatory variables. Specify the following options in the MODEL statement:

DWPROB option	computes the probability value for the Durbin-Watson *d* statistic.
NLAG= option	specifies how many autoregressive parameters to estimate in the model. For this example of a stepwise autoregressive model, you specify four autoregressive parameters initially.
BACKSTEP option	removes nonsignificant autoregressive parameters. The parameters are removed in order of least significance. The default significance level criterion used by the BACKSTEP option is 0.05. You can change this level using the SLSTAY= option.
METHOD= option	specifies the type of estimation method. In this example, you use maximum likelihood estimation.

The following SAS program produces the results shown in Output 6.15:

```
proc autoreg data=housecon;
   model hstarts=constr intrate / dwprob
                                  nlag=4
                                  backstep
                                  method=ml;
   run;
```

Output 6.15
Correcting for
Autocorrelation with
PROC AUTOREG

```
                            Construction Data                           1

                              Autoreg Procedure

      Dependent Variable = HSTARTS    Housing starts (in 1000s)


                        Ordinary Least Squares Estimates

                SSE          21621.29    DFE              79
                MSE          273.6873    Root MSE    16.5435
                SBC          703.0527    AIC         695.8325
                Reg Rsq        0.6515    Total Rsq     0.6515
        ❶       Durbin-Watson  0.8420    PROB<DW       0.0001


        Variable    DF      B Value    Std Error  t Ratio Approx Prob

        Intercept    1  -161.707523       26.403   -6.125      0.0001
        CONSTR       1  0.0074270744     0.000626   11.859      0.0001
        INTRATE      1    14.794782        1.675    8.832      0.0001


        Variable    DF  Variable Label

        Intercept    1
        CONSTR       1  Construction contracts (in $1,000,000)
        INTRATE      1  New home mortgage interest rate


                  ❷    Estimates of Autocorrelations

    Lag  Covariance  Correlation -1 9 8 7 6 5 4 3 2 1 0 1 2 3 4 5 6 7 8 9 1

     0   263.6743     1.000000  |                    |********************|
     1   146.5879     0.555943  |                    |**********          |
     2   130.0086     0.493065  |                    |**********          |
     3   96.36173     0.365457  |                    |*******             |
     4   62.07979     0.235441  |                    |*****               |


           ❸    Backward Elimination of Autoregressive Terms

                   Lag    Estimate    t-Ratio    Prob
                    3    -0.057559    -0.4643   0.6438
                    4     0.060324     0.5677   0.5719


                    Preliminary MSE = 169.2606

        ❹   Estimates of the Autoregressive Parameters

               Lag   Coefficient    Std Error    t Ratio
                1    -0.40789663    0.10984555  -3.713365
                2    -0.26629788    0.10984555  -2.424294
```

```
                            Construction Data                           2

                              Autoreg Procedure

                        Maximum Likelihood Estimates

                SSE          12813.32    DFE              77
                MSE          166.4067    Root MSE    12.89987
                SBC          669.7847    AIC         657.7511
                Reg Rsq        0.6607    Total Rsq     0.7934
        ❺       Durbin-Watson  2.0388    PROB<DW       0.5160


        Variable    DF      B Value    Std Error  t Ratio Approx Prob
❻
        Intercept    1  -114.225728       46.033   -2.481      0.0153
        CONSTR       1  0.007203297     0.000607   11.873      0.0001
        INTRATE      1    10.418202        3.943    2.642      0.0100
```

```
A(1)          1      -0.414704      0.110    -3.768      0.0003
A(2)          1      -0.359573      0.116    -3.103      0.0027


Variable     DF  Variable Label

Intercept     1
CONSTR        1  Construction contracts (in $1,000,000)
INTRATE       1  New home mortgage interest rate


            Autoregressive parameters assumed given.


Variable     DF      B Value    Std Error   t Ratio Approx Prob

Intercept     1   -114.225728      45.366    -2.518      0.0139
CONSTR        1    0.007203297   0.000589    12.239      0.0001
INTRATE       1     10.418202       3.893     2.676      0.0091


Variable     DF  Variable Label

Intercept     1
CONSTR        1  Construction contracts (in $1,000,000)
INTRATE       1  New home mortgage interest rate
```

Interpretation of output

The circled numbers on the output correspond to the numbers in the following list:

❶ The Durbin-Watson *d* statistic and its p-value are listed with the labels, Durbin-Watson and PROB<DW, respectively. Using ordinary least-squares estimates for the construction data, the *d* statistic has a value of 0.8420, with a p-value of 0.0001. You can conclude that these data are autocorrelated.

❷ PROC AUTOREG prints estimates of all the autocorrelations that you specify with the NLAG= option. In this example, because you specify NLAG=4, PROC AUTOREG estimates four autocorrelations.

❸ Backward Elimination of Autoregressive Terms shows that the third and fourth autoregressive parameters are removed from the model because their estimates are not statistically significant.

❹ Only the first two autoregressive parameter estimates are used to correct the model for autocorrelation.

❺ Under Maximum Likelihood Estimates, you can see that the Durbin-Watson statistic for the corrected model has a value of 2.0388 with a p-value of 0.5160. You can conclude that the two autoregressive parameters successfully correct the model for the autocorrelation present in the data.

❻ PROC AUTOREG lists the estimates for the explanatory variable parameters and the autoregressive parameters. All of the estimates are statistically significant at the 0.05 level. The final estimated model for the house construction data is expressed in the following equations:

$$HSTARTS_t = -114.23 + 0.0072CONSTR_t + 10.4182INTRATE_t + \nu_t$$

$$\nu_t = 0.4147\nu_{t-1} + 0.3596\nu_{t-2} + \epsilon_t \quad .$$

Note that the signs of the autoregressive parameters shown in this equation for ν_t are the reverse of the estimates shown in the PROC AUTOREG output.

Learning More

□ For more information on regression analysis using SAS software, see *SAS System for Regression, Second Edition.* Also, see Chapter 1, "Introduction to Regression Procedures," in the *SAS/STAT User's Guide, Version 6, Fourth Edition, Volume 1.*

□ For complete reference information on the CORR, MEANS, PLOT, PRINT, and UNIVARIATE procedures, see the *SAS Procedures Guide, Version 6, Third Edition.*

□ For complete reference information on the GPLOT procedure, see *SAS/GRAPH Software: Reference, Version 6, First Edition, Volume 1* and *Volume 2.*

□ For complete reference information on the LOGISTIC, REG, and TTEST procedures, and other procedures useful for regression analysis, see the *SAS/STAT User's Guide, Version 6, Fourth Edition, Volume 1* and *Volume 2.*

□ For complete reference information on the AUTOREG procedure, see the *SAS/ETS User's Guide, Version 6, Second Edition.*

□ For more examples and applications of correcting for autocorrelation using PROC AUTOREG and other procedures, see *SAS/ETS Software: Applications Guide 1, Version 6, First Edition* and *SAS/ETS Software: Applications Guide 2, Version 6, First Edition.*

References

□ Durbin, J. and Watson, G.S. (1951), "Testing for Serial Correlation in Least Squares Regression," *Biometrika*, 37, 409-428.

□ Johnston, J. (1984), *Econometric Methods*, Third Edition, New York: McGraw Hill Book Co.

□ Miller, R.G., Jr. (1981), *Simultaneous Statistical Inference*, New York: Springer-Verlag.

□ Pindyck, R.S. and Rubinfeld, D.L. (1991), *Econometric Models and Economic Forecasts*, Third Edition, New York: McGraw Hill Book Co.

□ U.S. Department of Commerce, Bureau of Economic Analysis (1990), *Survey of Current Business*, Washington, D.C.: U.S. Government Printing Office.

Chapter 7 Accessing Database Tables and Files

Introduction

This chapter introduces you to SAS/ACCESS software and its terminology and briefly describes how to use the interface. SAS/ACCESS software provides a link between the SAS System and data that you have stored in another software vendor's database table or file. For example, suppose you have information on a product's regional sales stored in an ORACLE database table. You can use SAS/ACCESS software to link that information to the SAS System so that you can use statistical procedures in SAS/STAT software or SAS/ETS software to analyze the data.

With SAS/ACCESS software, you can describe database tables and files to the SAS System. You store the description in SAS/ACCESS descriptor files, which you can use in SAS programs in much the same way as you would use SAS data files. You can print, plot, and chart the data described by the descriptor files, use them to create other SAS data sets, and so on.

SAS/ACCESS software provides interfaces to a variety of database management systems and PC files under many different operating systems. Refer to the "Learning More" section at the end of this chapter for a list of SAS/ACCESS documentation that describes the SAS/ACCESS interfaces currently available.

Overview of SAS/ACCESS Software

SAS/ACCESS software provides an interface between the SAS System and data from other software vendors' database management systems (DBMS), including PC file formats such as the DBF and DIF formats. The SAS/ACCESS interface consists of two procedures and an interface view engine, which perform the following tasks:

□ ACCESS procedure

    □ creates SAS/ACCESS descriptor files that describe data in the database table or file

    □ creates SAS data files from the database tables or files.

□ Interface View Engine

    □ enables you to use descriptor files to read database tables or files directly into SAS programs

    □ enables you to specify descriptor files in SAS programs to update, insert, or delete data in database tables or files.

□ DBLOAD procedure

    □ loads SAS data or other data into a database table or file.

The following sections describe SAS/ACCESS descriptor files and the ways you can use them to access data stored in database tables or files. These sections also describe the interface view engine, which actually sends and receives data between the SAS System and the database tables or files.

ACCESS Procedure: Creating and Using SAS/ACCESS Descriptor Files

SAS/ACCESS descriptor files are the tools the SAS System uses to establish a connection to a database product or PC file. To create descriptor files, use the ACCESS procedure.

There are two kinds of descriptor files: access descriptors and view descriptors. Figure 7.1 illustrates the relationships among a database product table or file, an access descriptor, and view descriptors. The following sections give a brief overview of the two types of descriptor files.

Figure 7.1
Relationships among a DBMS Table or File, an Access Descriptor, and View Descriptors

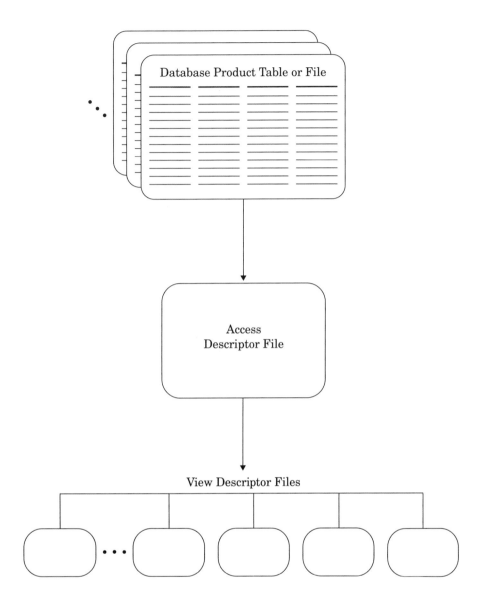

Access Descriptors

An *access descriptor* holds essential information about the DBMS table or file you want to access, for example, the table or file's name, column names, and data types. The access descriptor can also contain the corresponding SAS System information, such as the SAS variable names and formats. Typically, you have only one access descriptor for each table or file.

An access descriptor only describes the database table's or file's format and contents to the SAS System. You cannot use an access descriptor in a SAS program; rather, you use an access descriptor to create other SAS files, called view descriptors, that you use in SAS programs.

View Descriptors

A *view descriptor* defines some or all of the data described by one access descriptor (and, therefore, one DBMS table, view, or file). For example, you may want to use only three of four possible columns and only some of the rows. The view descriptor enables you to do this by selecting the fields or columns you want to use and specifying criteria to retrieve, group, or order only the rows that you want. You can have several view descriptors, which select different subsets of data for each access descriptor that you have defined.

A view descriptor is a SAS data set or, more specifically, a SAS data view.* You use a view descriptor in a SAS program much as you would any SAS data set. For example, you can specify a view descriptor in the DATA= statement of a SAS procedure or the SET statement of a DATA step. You can use a view descriptor in a SELECT statement of the SQL procedure to join, for example, the view descriptor's data with SAS data.

You can also use a view descriptor to update data directly in some of the DBMS tables or files. For example, you can specify a view descriptor to add or delete records in the database table or file or to change the values in a field using the FSEDIT or SQL procedure. You can also modify a database table or file by specifying a view descriptor in the MODIFY or REPLACE statement of a DATA step.

In some cases, you may also want to create a SAS data set from a database table or file. When you use a view descriptor to copy a database table or file into a SAS data set, it is called *extracting* the data. You can extract data in a number of ways. For example, you can extract data using various methods within the ACCESS procedure, a DATA step, or the OUT= option in a SAS procedure. When you need to use a database table or file in a number of procedures or DATA steps, extracting the data into a SAS data set may use fewer resources than directly accessing the data repeatedly.

Interface View Engine: Reading and Sending Data Transparently

All SAS data sets, including view descriptors, use a SAS engine to retrieve data. Each SAS/ACCESS interface has its own *interface view engine*, which enables the interface to retrieve or send data between the SAS System and a DBMS or PC file format. While the interface view engine is an integral part of the SAS/ACCESS interface, the interface's design is transparent, so you seldom have to deal directly with the engine. However, understanding how the engine works can help you modify your system configuration to improve performance.

The name of the interface view engine is stored in SAS/ACCESS descriptor files when you create them. When you specify a view descriptor in a SAS program, the SAS System automatically interacts with the interface view engine to access the database table or file. That is, every time you use a view descriptor to read data from a database table or file into a DATA step or modify that data using a SAS procedure, you are actually calling the interface view engine to access the data.

---

* See page 475 in *SAS Language and Procedures: Usage* for more information on Version 6 SAS data sets and how they are defined.

DBLOAD Procedure: Creating and Loading Database Tables and Files

The DBLOAD procedure enables you to create a new DBMS table or PC file and load it with data. The data can be read from any SAS data file, PROC SQL view, DATA step view, or view descriptor. The DBLOAD procedure gives you greater flexibility to retrieve and load data from any DBMS or PC file format to which you have a SAS/ACCESS interface.

Defining SAS/ACCESS Descriptor Files

To create and use SAS/ACCESS descriptor files, follow these steps:

1. Create an access descriptor.

2. Create a view descriptor based on the access descriptor.

3. Use the view descriptor to access the database table or file.

The examples in the following sections show how to create access descriptors for a few types of software vendors' products.

You begin by using the SAS LIBNAME statement to associate *librefs* with the SAS data libraries in which you want to store the descriptors. You can have one library for access descriptors and a separate library for view descriptors, or you can put both access descriptors and view descriptors in the same data library. Having separate libraries for access and view descriptors helps you maintain data security by enabling you to control separately who can read and update each type of descriptor.

Creating an Access Descriptor

To create an access descriptor, follow these steps:

1. Open the ACCESS window.

2. Specify the access descriptor name in the ACCESS window.

3. Select the interface view engine in the Engine Selection window.

4. Identify the table or file for the access descriptor in the Access Descriptor Identification window.

5. Customize the access descriptor using the Access Descriptor Display window.

Opening the ACCESS Window

To open the ACCESS window, select **Access** from the **Globals** menu of the SAS Display Manager System PROGRAM EDITOR window, or submit the following SAS statements from the PROGRAM EDITOR window:

```
proc access;
run;
```

The ACCESS window lists all the files associated with any LIBNAME statements you submit. Each file is listed with its libref (or libname), member name, member type (such as

CATALOG, ACCESS, VIEW, or DATA), and information specifying whether any SAS indexes are defined on variables in the SAS data files. Note that these are indexes defined through the SAS System and are not to be confused with any DBMS indexes. Display 7.1 shows an example of an ACCESS window after an access descriptor and a view descriptor have been created.

Display 7.1
ACCESS Window
Example

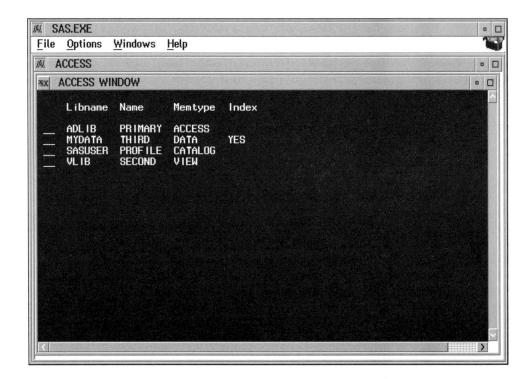

Specifying the Access Descriptor Name

After opening the ACCESS window, specify the name of the access descriptor you want to create.

To specify an access descriptor with the two-level name ADLIB.CUSTOMER, follow these steps:

1. Select **New** from the **File** menu to open the New window.

2. Type **ADLIB** and **CUSTOMER** in the **LIBREF** and **NAME** fields, respectively. The type **ACCESS** is automatically supplied to indicate you are creating an access descriptor.

3. Select **OK** (or press ENTER) to create the access descriptor and go to the Engine Selection window.

    Display 7.2 shows an example of a filled-in New window.

Display 7.2
New Window
Example

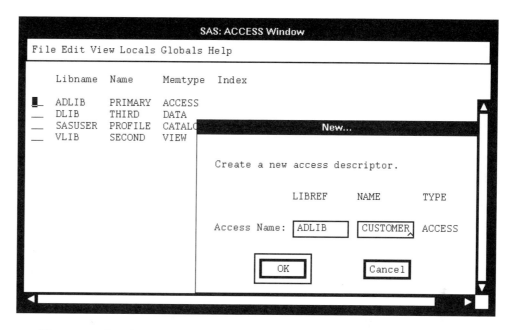

If an access descriptor with this name already exists, you get a warning message to this effect when you open the Access Descriptor Identification window later. If you continue creating the new version of the descriptor, the old version is overwritten when the new version is saved.

Selecting the Interface View Engine

The Engine Selection window lists all available Version 6 SAS/ACCESS interface products that you have licensed for your operating system. To choose an interface view engine, select the line describing your desired interface view engine. This opens the Access Descriptor Identification window. Display 7.3 shows an example of the Engine Selection window with a few software vendor products listed.

Display 7.3
Engine Selection
Window Example

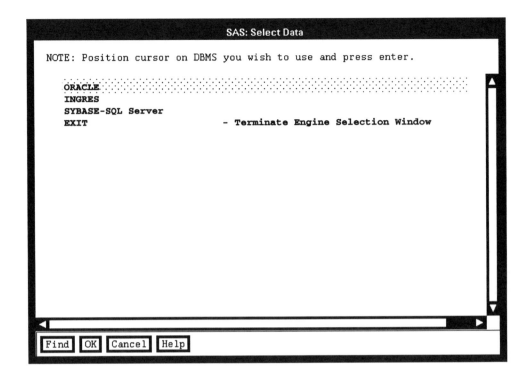

Access Descriptor Identification Window

The Access Descriptor Identification window has a different appearance depending on which interface view engine you select. Displays 7.4, 7.5, and 7.6 show examples of the Access Descriptor Identification window as it appears for ORACLE, IBM AS/400, and the DBF PC file format, respectively.

Display 7.4
Example of the
Access Descriptor
Identification
Window for
ORACLE

```
                        SAS: ACCESS: Create Descriptor
  ┌──────────────────────────────────────────────────────────────────────┐
  │ Globals Help                                                           │
  ├──────────────────────────────────────────────────────────────────────┤
  │                                                                        │
  │            ORACLE Access Descriptor Identification Window              │
  │                                                                        │
  │                                                                        │
  │   Descriptor: Library: ADLIB      Member: CUSTOMER    Type: ACCESS     │
  │                                                                        │
  │   Assign Names: NO                                                     │
  │                                                                        │
  │   Table:       █                                                       │
  │   User Name:                                                           │
  │   Password:                                                            │
  │   Path:                                                                │
  │                                                                        │
  │                                                                        │
  │                                                                        │
```

Display 7.5
Example of the
Access Descriptor
Identification
Window for AS/400

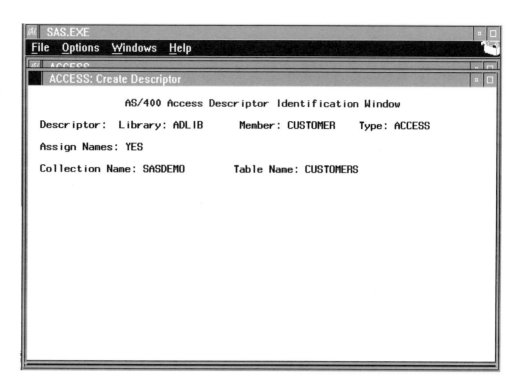

Display 7.6
Example of the
Access Descriptor
Identification
Window for DBF
Files

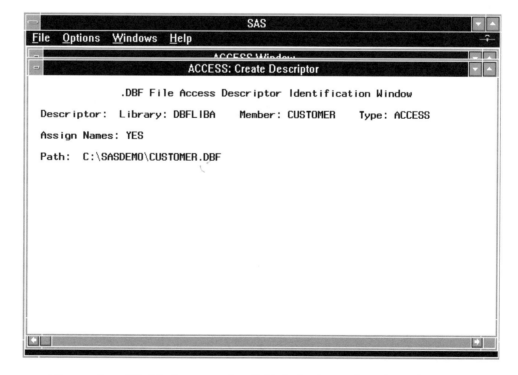

After you have filled in the appropriate fields in the Access Descriptor Identification window, press ENTER. If a field is in error, it is highlighted, and a message window appears that includes a description of the error. Press ENTER again to return to the display, where you can correct the error. If all the fields are correct, the information is processed, and the Access Descriptor Display window appears.

Access Descriptor Display Window

The Access Descriptor Display window has a different appearance depending on which interface view engine you select. Displays 7.7, 7.8, and 7.9 show examples of the Access Descriptor Display window as it appears before you modify it for ORACLE, AS/400, and DBF files, respectively.

Display 7.7
Example of the
Access Descriptor
Display Window for
ORACLE

```
                    SAS: ACCESS: Create Descriptor

 Locals Globals Help

                ORACLE Access Descriptor Display Window

  Descriptor: Library: ADLIB       Member: CUSTOMER    Type: ACCESS

  Table:     CUSTOMERS
  User Name: SCOTT
  PATH:
  "@orav7sn2"


    Func  Sel  Column Name                   Sas Name  Format

     _     *   CUSTOMER                      CUSTOMER  $8.
     _     *   STATE                         STATE     $2.
     _     *   ZIPCODE                       ZIPCODE   $5.
     _     *   COUNTRY                       COUNTRY   $20.
     _     *   TELEPHONE                     TELEPHON  $12.
     _     *   NAME                          NAME      $60.
     _     *   CONTACT                       CONTACT   $30.
     _     *   STREETADDRESS                 STREETAD  $40.
     _     *   CITY                          CITY      $25.
     _     *   FIRSTORDERDATE                FIRSTORD  DATETIME16.
```

Display 7.8
*Example of the
Access Descriptor
Display Window for
AS/400*

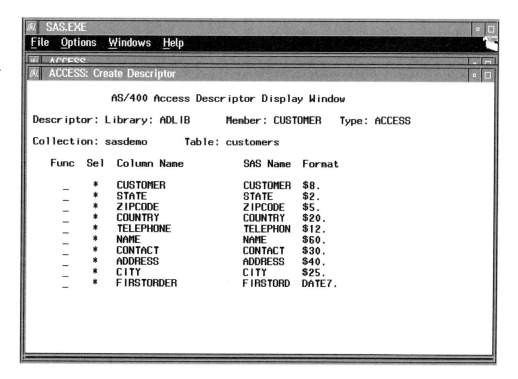

Display 7.9
*Example of the
Access Descriptor
Display Window for
DBF Files*

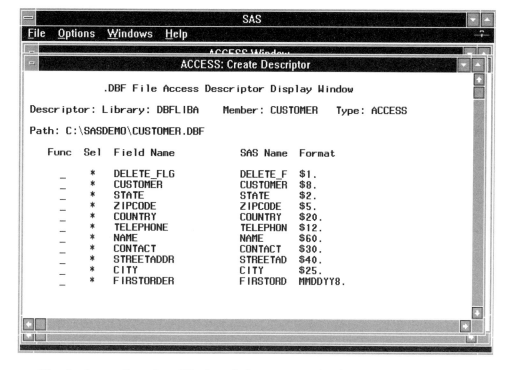

Use the Access Descriptor Display window to customize the access descriptor you created. For example, you can type D (for Drop) in the Func field for each column that you want to make unavailable for selection when creating view descriptors. However, each column so marked will continue to be in the access descriptor and in the DBMS table. You can also type over the SAS names to give the variables new names, and you can type over the formats to change them.

After you have customized your access descriptor, you are ready to store it. To store the access descriptor and return to the Access Descriptor Identification window, select **End** from the **Locals** menu.[*]

Creating a View Descriptor

Just as you supplied the specifications for an access descriptor in the Access Descriptor Display window, you supply the specifications for a view descriptor in the View Descriptor Display window. There are two methods to get to the View Descriptor Display window:

□ Use the PROC ACCESS statement with no options to open the ACCESS window. Once you are in the ACCESS window, place your cursor in the selection field beside the desired access descriptor. Type **CV** (for Create View) and press ENTER.

□ Use the PROC ACCESS statement with the ACCDESC= option, which specifies the two-level name of the access descriptor to be used to create the view descriptor.

The View Descriptor Display window appears next. The structure of the View Descriptor Display window depends on the interface view engine you select. See the documentation for the relevant interface for more details on filling in the View Descriptor Display window. Displays 7.10, 7.11, and 7.12 show examples of the View Descriptor Display window as it first appears for ORACLE, AS/400, and DBF files, respectively.

---

[*]You can issue the END command in several ways, including the following: select the **End** command from the first menu on the display; press a function key defined for that purpose; double-click on the window's system icon; or enter the END command on a Command line.

Display 7.10
Example of the View
Descriptor Display
Window for
ORACLE

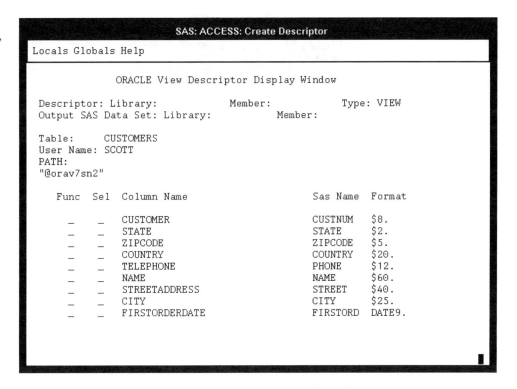

Display 7.11
Example of the View
Descriptor Display
Window for AS/400

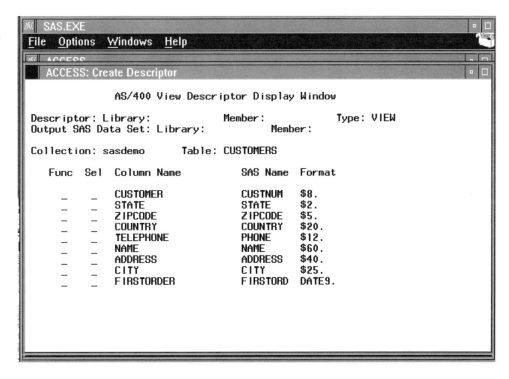

Display 7.12
Example of the View
Descriptor Display
Window for DBF
Files

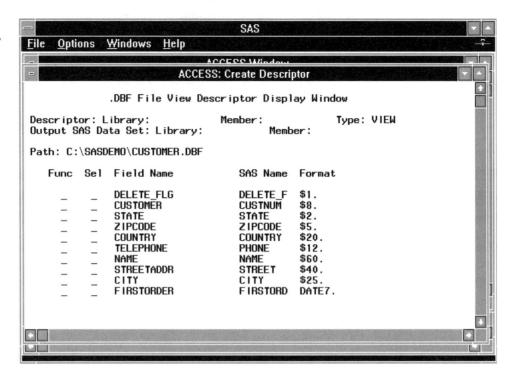

Here you choose columns to be included in the view descriptor. Type **S** (for Select) in the **Func** field for each column that you want to include in the view descriptor.

Select the **End** command from the **Locals** menu to save the view descriptor. If a field is in error, it is highlighted, and a message window appears that includes a description of the error. Press ENTER again to return to the display, where you can correct the error. If all the fields are correct, the view descriptor is saved, and you return to the ACCESS window.

Using Procedure Statements to Create Descriptors

This section presents some examples of creating access descriptors and view descriptors using PROC ACCESS statements and options. You can submit these examples from the PROGRAM EDITOR window, or you can put the examples in a program and submit it for batch processing.

Creating Access and View Descriptors in One PROC Step

Perhaps the most common way to use the ACCESS procedure is to create an access descriptor and one or more view descriptors in a single PROC ACCESS execution.

The following example creates an access descriptor ADLIB.INVOICE, based on the ORACLE table **invoice**. Two view descriptors are created, VLIB.EXCHRATE and VLIB.NOPAYMT, based on this access descriptor. Each SAS/ACCESS statement is then explained in the order it appears in the example program.

```
libname adlib 'SAS-data-library';
libname vlib 'SAS-data-library';
```

```
proc access dbms=oracle;
   create adlib.invoice.access;
      path="@orav7sn2";
      user=rich;
      orapw=money;
      table=invoice;
      assign=yes;
      rename invoicenum=invnum amtbilled=amtbilld amountinus=amtinus;
      format amtbilled dollar18.2 amountinus dollar18.2;
      list all;

   create vlib.exchrate.view;
      select invoicenum billedon billedto country amtbilled amountinus;
   create vlib.nopaymt.view;
      select invoicenum billedto amountinus billedon;
      subset where country='USA' and paidon < '01-JAN-94';
run;
```

Here is an explanation of the statements in this example:

`libname adlib` '*SAS-data-library*';
`libname vlib` '*SAS-data-library*';
uses LIBNAME statements to associate the librefs ADLIB and VLIB with their respective SAS data libraries. You must associate a libref with its data library before you use it in another SAS statement or procedure.

`proc access dbms=oracle;`
invokes the ACCESS procedure for the SAS/ACCESS interface to ORACLE.

`create adlib.invoice.access;`
identifies the access descriptor, ADLIB.INVOICE, that you want to create.

`path=''@orav7sn2'';`
identifies an alias for an ORACLE two-task device driver, node, and database. The path argument must be enclosed in double quotes to preserve case-sensitivity in a UNIX environment.

`user=rich;`
identifies the ORACLE user name.

`orapw=money;`
identifies the user's password on the ORACLE database.

`table=invoice;`
specifies the ORACLE table named **`invoice`** on which the access descriptor is to be created.

`assign=yes;`
generates unique SAS variable names from the first eight characters (including blanks) of the ORACLE column names. SAS variable formats are generated automatically from the columns' SQL data types. These variable names and formats can be changed in this access descriptor but not in any view descriptors created from this access descriptor.

`rename invoicenum=invnum amtbilled=amtbilld amountinus=amtinus;`
renames the SAS variables associated with the **`invoicenum`**, **`amtbilled`**, and **`amountinus`** columns. Because the **`assign=yes`** statement is specified, any view

descriptors created from this access descriptor automatically use the new SAS variable names.

format amtbilled dollar18.2 amountinus dollar18.2;
assigns the SAS format DOLLAR18.2 to the SAS variables associated with the **amtbilled** and **amountinus** columns. You specify the ORACLE column names in this statement. Because the **assign=yes** statement is specified, any view descriptors created from this access descriptor automatically use the new SAS variable formats. Use of an equal sign in this statement is optional.

list all;
lists the access descriptor's columns, variables, and formats in the SAS log. Any columns that have been dropped from display (using the DROP statement) are listed in the SAS log as *NON-DISPLAY*.

create vlib.exchrate.view;
identifies the view descriptor, VLIB.EXCHRATE, that you want to create, and it causes the previous access descriptor to be written.

select invoicenum billedon billedto country amtbilled amountinus;
selects the **invoicenum, billedon, billedto, country, amtbilled,** and **amountinus** columns for inclusion in a view descriptor. The SELECT statement is required to create the view. You specify the ORACLE column names in this statement.

create vlib.nopaymt.view;
identifies the next view descriptor, VLIB.NOPAYMT, that you want to create, and it causes the previous view descriptor to be written.

select invoicenum billedto amountinus billedon;
selects the **invoicenum, billedto, amountinus,** and **billedon** columns for inclusion in a view descriptor.

subset where country='USA' and paidon < '01-JAN-94';
specifies you want the view descriptor to include only observations for companies based in the U.S. who have not paid their invoices by January 1, 1994. You specify the ORACLE SQL WHERE clause syntax and column names in this statement.

run;
writes the last view descriptor when the RUN statement is processed.

Reviewing and Editing Descriptor Files

After you have created the SAS/ACCESS descriptor files, you can review or edit them. To browse an access descriptor or a view descriptor, use the BD (browse descriptor) selection-field command in the ACCESS window. Place your cursor in the selection field beside the access descriptor or view descriptor that you want to browse, type **BD**, and press ENTER. An Access Descriptor Display window or a View Descriptor Display window will appear. To edit an access descriptor or a view descriptor, follow the previous steps, but type **ED** (edit descriptor) in the selection field instead of **BD**.

Using the ACCESS Procedure to Extract Data

If you are using the same data repeatedly in several SAS jobs, it is less resource-intensive to access the extracted data in a SAS data set than it is to access the data repeatedly from the database table or file.

There are several methods of extracting data, including the Extract a view window in the ACCESS window, the PROC ACCESS statement options, and the View Descriptor Display window. These three methods are described in the following sections. If you use the PROC ACCESS statement options, you can extract the data in batch mode.

Extracting with the Extract a View Window

To extract data from a view descriptor and place them into a SAS data file, go to the ACCESS window. Select **Open** from the **File** menu. Then select **Extract a view** from the second menu that appears.

The Extract a view window appears on your display. Display 7.13 shows an example of a completed Extract a view window.

Display 7.13
Extract a View
Window Example

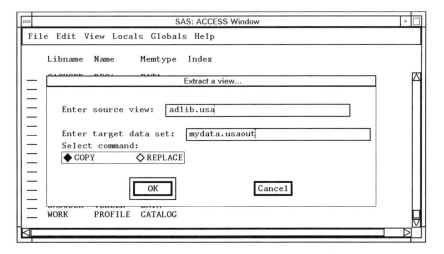

At the **Enter source view** prompt, enter the name of the view descriptor that describes the data you want to extract. You should use the two-level name that specifies the view descriptor's libref and member name, for example, **ADLIB.USA**. At the **Enter the target data set** prompt, enter the name of the output SAS data file. Use the SAS data file's two-level name, for example, **MYDATA.USAOUT**. A libref must be associated with a SAS data library before you can use it for an output data file.

The window also asks you whether you are copying the view's data into the data file (the default) or whether you are replacing the data in the file. If you want to overwrite an existing SAS data file, choose the REPLACE command.

Extracting with PROC ACCESS Statement Options

To extract data from the view descriptor ADLIB.USA using only the PROC ACCESS statement options, submit the following statements from display manager's PROGRAM EDITOR window:

```
proc access viewdesc=adlib.usa out=mydata.usaout;
run;
```

ADLIB.USA is the two-level name that specifies the libref and member name for the view descriptor that describes the data you want to extract. MYDATA.USAOUT is the two-level name that specifies the libref and member name for the output SAS data file.

This method of extracting data can be used in batch mode, which is useful for extracting large amounts of data. Although your current process is occupied in this mode, you can open another process and continue other work until the extraction is complete.

Extracting with the View Descriptor Display Window

You can extract data using the `Output SAS Data Set: Library` and `Member` fields in the View Descriptor Display window. This method of extracting data is the most efficient if you want to extract the data at the same time you create the view descriptor.

When you select **End** from the `Locals` menu, the view descriptor is created at the same time that the data are extracted. This extraction is only performed once. If you edit the view descriptor after you create it, the `Output SAS Data Set: Library` and `Member` fields are blank when the View Descriptor Display window appears.

Creating and Loading Database Tables and Files

You use the DBLOAD procedure to create and load database tables or files. You can use the DBLOAD procedure to create and load database tables or files from a SAS data set, from a view descriptor created with the DATA step or the SQL procedure, or from a view descriptor created with the ACCESS procedure.

When you use the DBLOAD procedure to create a database data file and load it with data, the DBLOAD procedure associates each SAS variable in the input data with a column in the database table or file and assigns a default name and data type to each column. You can use the default information or change column names and data types as necessary. When you finish customizing the columns, the DBLOAD procedure creates the database table or file and loads it with data.

To create and load a database table or file using display manager mode, submit the PROC DBLOAD and RUN statements from the PROGRAM EDITOR window of the SAS Display Manager System.

```
proc dbload;
run;
```

The Engine Selection window appears next, asking you to choose the interface view engine you want to use. When this window appears, click on the line that lists the desired interface view engine to open the Load Identification window.

You can also run the DBLOAD procedure in interactive line mode or batch mode. See the documentation for the relevant interface for more information on using these methods.

Load Identification Window

Use the Load Identification window to identify the name of the input data and to specify the database table or file you want to create. The appearance of the Load Identification Window depends on the interface view engine you select. Displays 7.14 and 7.15 show examples of a Load Identification window for ORACLE and DBF files, respectively.

Display 7.14
Example of the Load Identification Window for ORACLE

```
                                    SAS: DBLOAD:
  Locals Globals Help

                    ORACLE Load Identification Window

  Input Data:                        Access Descriptor:

  Input Limit: 5000


  User Name:

  Password:

  Table Name:

  Tablespace:

  Path:


  Commit Frequency: 1000      Error Limit: 100
```

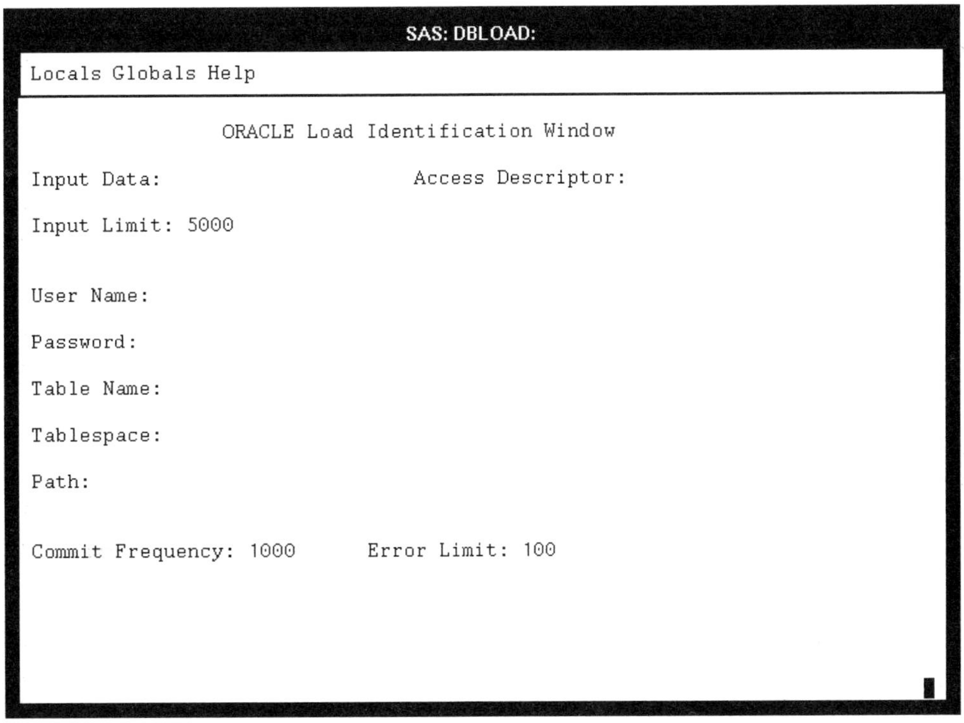

Display 7.15
Example of the Load
Identification
Window for DBF
Files

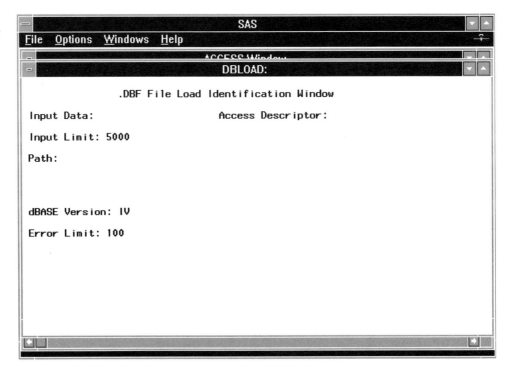

When you have entered all the necessary information, press ENTER. If a field is in error, it is highlighted, and a message window appears that includes a description of the error. Press ENTER again to return to the display, where you can correct the error. If all the fields are correct, the information is processed, and the Load Display window appears.

Load Display Window

Use the Load Display window to specify the column names and data types associated with each SAS variable in the input data. Type D (for Drop) in the Func field for each column that you want to drop from the new table. Type over any column (field) names and column (field) types that you want to change. As with the Load Identification window, the appearance of the Load Display Window depends on the interface view engine you select. Displays 7.16 and 7.17 show examples of a Load Display window for ORACLE and DBF files, respectively.

Display 7.16
Example of a Load
Display Window for
ORACLE

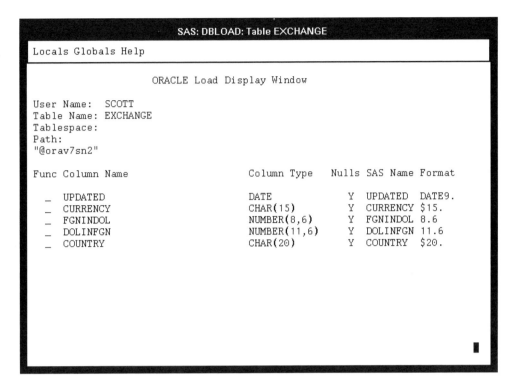

Display 7.17
Example of the Load
Display Window for
DBF Files

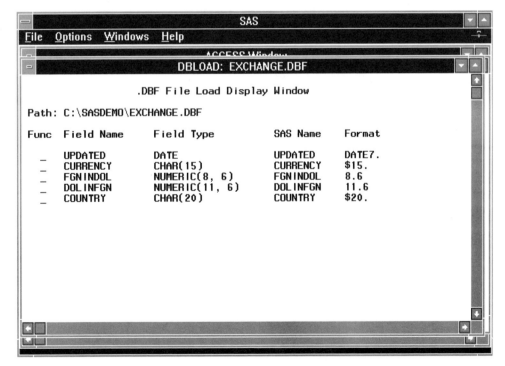

When you have finished, select **End** from the **Locals** menu. The SAS System checks
for errors, for example, an incompatible data type. If an entry is invalid, it is highlighted, and

a message window appears describing the error. Press ENTER to return to the display to correct the error. Select **End** again.

To load the table or file, select **Load** from the **Locals** menu. If you want to cancel the load, select **Cancel** instead of **Load**. If the number of inserted observations is very large, you may want to cancel the load and resubmit it as a batch job. If you are sure you want to load the table or file, you can bypass the earlier message by selecting **Load** without first selecting **End** from the **Locals** menu.

Learning More

The following interface guides explain how to use SAS/ACCESS software with various software vendors' products. They explain how to create SAS/ACCESS descriptor files and provide information on using them in SAS programs. For a complete list of SAS/ACCESS interface guides, consult the *Publications Catalog*.

□ *SAS/ACCESS Interface to ADABAS: Usage and Reference, Version 6, First Edition*

□ *SAS/ACCESS Interface to AS/400 Data: Usage and Reference, Version 6, First Edition*

□ *SAS/ACCESS Interface to CA-DATACOM/DB: Usage and Reference, Version 6, First Edition*

□ *SAS/ACCESS Interface to DB2: Usage and Reference, Version 6, First Edition*

□ *SAS/ACCESS Interface to IMS-DL/I: Usage and Reference, Version 6, First Edition*

□ *SAS/ACCESS Interface to INGRES: Usage and Reference, Version 6, First Edition*

□ *SAS/ACCESS Interface to ORACLE: Usage and Reference, Version 6, Second Edition*

□ *SAS/ACCESS Interface to OS/2 Database Products: Usage and Reference, Version 6, First Edition*

□ *SAS/ACCESS Interface to PC File Formats: Usage and Reference, Version 6, First Edition*

□ *SAS/ACCESS Interface to Rdb/VMS: Usage and Reference, Version 6, First Edition*

□ *SAS/ACCESS Interface to SQL/DS: Usage and Reference, Version 6, First Edition*

□ *SAS/ACCESS Interface to SYBASE and SQL Server: Usage and Reference, Version 6, First Edition*

□ *SAS/ACCESS Interface to SYSTEM 2000 Data Management Software: Usage and Reference, Version 6, First Edition*

The following technical reports contain information on new developments in SAS/ACCESS software.

□ SAS Technical Report P-221, *SAS/ACCESS Software: Changes and Enhancements, Release 6.07* describes new features and changes to Release 6.07 of the following SAS/ACCESS interfaces: ADABAS, CA-DATACOM/DB, DB2, ORACLE, Rdb/VMS, SQL/DS, and SYSTEM 2000. It also provides information on the SQL Procedure Pass-Through facility for the following interfaces: DB2, ORACLE, Rdb/VMS, and SQL/DS.

□ SAS Technical Report P-252, *SAS Software: Changes and Enhancements, Release 6.09* provides the latest features and changes to Release 6.09 of SAS software. It includes a description of the SQL Procedure Pass-Through facility for the SAS/ACCESS interface to INGRES when it runs under UNIX systems.

□ SAS Technical Report P-262, *SAS/ACCESS Interface to ODBC: SQL Procedure Pass-Through Facility, Release 6.08* provides information on the SQL Procedure Pass-Through facility for the SAS/ACCESS interface to ODBC.

Sample SAS® Data Sets

Car Sales Data

Use the following DATA step to produce the car sales data used in Chapter 4:

```
data carsales;
   title 'Car Sales Data';
   title2 'Prospective Sales Figures';
   length region $ 9;
   format revenue dollar10.0;
   label region='Region'
         statenm='State'
         style='Style'
         quantity='Sales Quantity'
         revenue='Sales Revenue (in $1000)';
   input region $ statenm $ style $ quantity revenue;
   cards;
Midwest     IA      coupe     200     3671
Midwest     IA      sedan     252     3863
Midwest     IA      wagon     263     4362
Midwest     IL      coupe     374     6964
Midwest     IL      sedan     485     7493
Midwest     IL      wagon     188     3111
Midwest     IN      coupe     330     6111
Midwest     IN      sedan     123     1890
Midwest     IN      wagon     108     1748
Midwest     MI      coupe     163     3003
Midwest     MI      sedan     486     7508
Midwest     MI      wagon     167     2749
Midwest     MN      coupe     200     3670
Midwest     MN      sedan     253     3865
Midwest     MN      wagon     174     2862
Midwest     MO      coupe     366     6588
Midwest     MO      sedan     506     7806
Midwest     MO      wagon     180     2907
Midwest     OH      coupe     238     4321
Midwest     OH      sedan     408     6164
Midwest     OH      wagon     275     4491
Midwest     WI      coupe     166     3004
Midwest     WI      sedan     312     4755
Midwest     WI      wagon     259     4211
Northeast   CT      coupe     348     6249
Northeast   CT      sedan     459     7124
Northeast   CT      wagon     179     2924
```

Northeast	MA	coupe	138	2577
Northeast	MA	sedan	469	7161
Northeast	MA	wagon	99	1593
Northeast	ME	coupe	226	4104
Northeast	ME	sedan	313	4840
Northeast	ME	wagon	123	2040
Northeast	NH	coupe	390	7177
Northeast	NH	sedan	427	6595
Northeast	NH	wagon	171	2837
Northeast	NJ	coupe	148	2738
Northeast	NJ	sedan	420	6377
Northeast	NJ	wagon	112	1850
Northeast	NY	coupe	297	5448
Northeast	NY	sedan	511	7774
Northeast	NY	wagon	114	1875
Northeast	PA	coupe	194	3601
Northeast	PA	sedan	223	3381
Northeast	PA	wagon	66	1080
Northeast	RI	coupe	303	5514
Northeast	RI	sedan	198	3065
Northeast	RI	wagon	229	3787
Northeast	VT	coupe	338	6276
Northeast	VT	sedan	267	4103
Northeast	VT	wagon	232	3782
South	AL	coupe	319	5831
South	AL	sedan	390	5983
South	AL	wagon	183	2983
South	AR	coupe	339	6246
South	AR	sedan	235	3625
South	AR	wagon	166	2738
South	DC	coupe	112	2099
South	DC	sedan	159	2438
South	DC	wagon	67	1077
South	DE	coupe	314	5696
South	DE	sedan	302	4612
South	DE	wagon	138	2248
South	FL	coupe	347	6302
South	FL	sedan	417	6344
South	FL	wagon	272	4500
South	GA	coupe	296	5312
South	GA	sedan	515	7792
South	GA	wagon	108	1790
South	KY	coupe	275	4929
South	KY	sedan	521	7922
South	KY	wagon	263	4244
South	LA	coupe	306	5630
South	LA	sedan	350	5347
South	LA	wagon	222	3635
South	MD	coupe	316	5659
South	MD	sedan	275	4203
South	MD	wagon	228	3670
South	MS	coupe	361	6623
South	MS	sedan	526	8105

South	MS	wagon	133	2146
South	NC	coupe	292	5339
South	NC	sedan	353	5380
South	NC	wagon	126	2059
South	SC	coupe	297	5335
South	SC	sedan	231	3501
South	SC	wagon	124	2026
South	TN	coupe	358	6444
South	TN	sedan	267	4081
South	TN	wagon	166	2726
South	VA	coupe	260	4836
South	VA	sedan	395	6116
South	VA	wagon	237	3916
South	WV	coupe	174	3129
South	WV	sedan	343	5307
South	WV	wagon	99	1627
West	AK	coupe	191	3528
West	AK	sedan	87	1367
West	AK	wagon	66	1100
West	AZ	coupe	180	3305
West	AZ	sedan	214	3241
West	AZ	wagon	87	1414
West	CA	coupe	175	3200
West	CA	sedan	238	3168
West	CA	wagon	62	989
West	CO	coupe	194	3604
West	CO	sedan	157	2411
West	CO	wagon	135	2178
West	HI	coupe	151	2701
West	HI	sedan	152	2305
West	HI	wagon	81	1329
West	ID	coupe	169	3095
West	ID	sedan	138	2081
West	ID	wagon	137	2271
West	KS	coupe	105	1893
West	KS	sedan	131	2002
West	KS	wagon	60	982
West	MT	coupe	189	3500
West	MT	sedan	143	2200
West	MT	wagon	51	845
West	ND	coupe	187	3454
West	ND	sedan	175	2698
West	ND	wagon	52	842
West	NE	coupe	106	1941
West	NE	sedan	109	1654
West	NE	wagon	124	2056
West	NM	coupe	56	1046
West	NM	sedan	83	1246
West	NM	wagon	106	1732
West	NV	coupe	70	1293
West	NV	sedan	190	2884
West	NV	wagon	106	1715
West	OK	coupe	67	1210

```
West       OK       sedan      152      2320
West       OK       wagon      110      1763
West       OR       coupe       99      1812
West       OR       sedan      172      2614
West       OR       wagon       97      1561
West       SD       coupe      176      3207
West       SD       sedan      148      2243
West       SD       wagon       66      1074
West       TX       coupe      126      2285
West       TX       sedan      154      2361
West       TX       wagon      140      2304
West       UT       coupe       54       973
West       UT       sedan      145      2218
West       UT       wagon       74      1211
West       WA       coupe      192      3469
West       WA       sedan       90      1378
West       WA       wagon      138      2279
West       WY       coupe       90      1672
West       WY       sedan      153      2329
West       WY       wagon       58       955
;
```

Airline Cost Data

Use the following DATA step to produce the airline cost data used in Chapter 6:

```
data airline;
   title 'Airline Cost Data';
   label cpm='Cost per mile'
         alf='Average load factor'
         asl='Average flight length'
         spa='Average seats per aircraft'
         utl='Average hours per day use of aircraft';
   input cpm alf asl spa utl;
   cards;
3.306 .287 1.528 .3522  8.09
3.527 .349 2.189 .3279  9.56
3.959 .362 1.518 .1356 10.80
4.737 .378 0.821 .1290  5.65
3.096 .381 1.692 .3007 10.20
3.689 .394 0.949 .1488  7.94
2.357 .397 3.607 .3390 13.30
2.833 .400 1.495 .3597  8.42
3.313 .405 0.863 .1390  9.57
3.044 .409 0.845 .1390  9.00
2.846 .410 0.840 .1390  9.62
2.341 .412 1.350 .1920  7.91
2.780 .417 2.377 .3287  8.83
3.392 .422 1.031 .1365  8.35
3.856 .425 2.780 .1282 10.60
3.462 .426 0.975 .2025  7.52
2.711 .434 1.912 .3148  8.36
```

```
2.743 .439 1.584 .1607  8.43
3.760 .452 1.164 .1270  7.55
3.311 .455 1.236 .1221  7.70
2.404 .466 1.123 .1481  9.38
2.962 .476 0.961 .1236  8.91
3.437 .476 1.416 .1145  7.27
2.906 .478 1.392 .1148  8.71
3.140 .486 0.877 .1060  8.29
2.275 .488 2.515 .3546  9.50
2.954 .495 0.871 .1186  8.44
3.306 .504 1.408 .1345  9.47
2.425 .535 1.576 .1361 10.80
2.971 .539 1.008 .1150  6.84
4.024 .541 0.823 .0943  6.31
2.363 .582 1.963 .1381  8.48
2.258 .591 1.790 .1375  7.87
;
```

House Construction Data

Use the following DATA step to produce the house construction data used in Chapter 6:

```
data housecon;
   title 'Construction Data';
   label date='Date'
         constr='Construction contracts (in $1,000,000)'
         intrate='New home mortgage interest rate'
         hstarts='Housing starts (in 1000s)';
   input date:monyy5. constr intrate hstarts;
   format date monyy5.;
   cards;
JAN83    11358    13.00    91.3
FEB83    11355    12.62    96.3
MAR83    16100    12.97   134.6
APR83    16315    12.02   135.8
MAY83    19205    12.21   174.9
JUN83    20263    11.90   173.2
JUL83    16885    12.02   161.6
AUG83    19441    12.01   176.8
SEP83    17379    12.08   154.9
OCT83    16028    11.80   159.3
NOV83    15401    11.82   136.0
DEC83    13518    11.94   108.3
JAN84    14023    11.80   109.1
FEB84    14442    11.78   130.0
MAR84    17916    11.56   137.5
APR84    17655    11.55   172.7
MAY84    21990    11.68   180.7
JUN84    20036    11.61   184.0
JUL84    19224    11.91   162.1
AUG84    19367    11.89   147.4
SEP84    16923    12.03   148.5
```

OCT84	18413	12.27	152.3
NOV84	16616	12.27	126.2
DEC84	14220	12.05	98.9
JAN85	15154	11.77	105.4
FEB85	13652	11.74	95.8
MAR85	20004	11.42	145.2
APR85	20692	11.55	176.0
MAY85	22532	11.55	170.5
JUN85	20043	11.31	163.4
JUL85	22047	10.94	160.7
AUG85	21055	10.78	160.7
SEP85	20541	10.69	147.7
OCT85	21715	10.64	173.0
NOV85	17691	10.55	124.1
DEC85	16276	10.47	120.5
JAN86	15417	10.40	115.6
FEB86	16152	10.21	107.2
MAR86	19617	10.04	151.0
APR86	23754	9.87	188.2
MAY86	23050	9.84	186.6
JUN86	23740	9.74	183.6
JUL86	23621	9.89	172.0
AUG86	21884	9.84	163.8
SEP86	21763	9.74	154.0
OCT86	21862	9.57	154.8
NOV86	17998	9.45	115.6
DEC86	17982	9.28	113.0
JAN87	16694	9.14	105.1
FEB87	15729	8.87	102.8
MAR87	22622	8.77	141.2
APR87	23077	8.84	159.3
MAY87	22054	8.99	158.0
JUN87	25703	9.05	162.9
JUL87	24567	9.01	152.4
AUG87	23836	9.01	143.6
SEP87	22418	9.03	152.0
OCT87	23360	8.86	139.1
NOV87	18663	8.92	118.8
DEC87	19224	8.78	85.4
JAN88	15113	8.75	78.2
FEB88	17496	8.76	90.2
MAR88	22257	8.77	128.8
APR88	22344	8.76	153.2
MAY88	24138	8.59	140.2
JUN88	26940	8.90	150.2
JUL88	22309	8.80	137.0
AUG88	24826	8.68	136.8
SEP88	22670	8.90	131.1
OCT88	22223	8.77	135.1
NOV88	19767	9.05	113.0
DEC88	19125	9.04	94.2
JAN89	15776	9.20	100.1
FEB89	15086	9.46	85.8

```
MAR89    21080     9.63   117.8
APR89    21725     9.88   129.4
MAY89    23796     9.82   131.7
JUN89    24650    10.09   143.2
JUL89    22330    10.06   134.7
AUG89    24128     9.83   122.4
SEP89    23371     9.87   109.3
OCT89    22669     9.77   130.3
;
```

Glossary

access descriptor
a SAS/ACCESS file that describes data to the SAS System that are in a database table or file. You use an access descriptor as a master descriptor file from which to create view descriptors.

alpha level
a fixed cutoff level of probability that is used to determine the significance of a statistical test. For example, if the alpha level is set at .05, then an observed p-value of .05 or less indicates that the test is statistically significant.

automatic variable
a variable that is created automatically by the DATA step, some DATA step statements, some SAS procedures, and the SAS macro facility.

base SAS software
software that includes a programming language that manages your data, procedures for data analysis and reporting, procedures for managing SAS files, a macro facility, help menus, and a windowing environment for text editing and file management.

catalog
See SAS catalog.

cell
a single unit of a table produced by a SAS procedure, such as the TABULATE or FREQ procedure. The value contained in the cell is a summary statistic for the input data set. The contents of the cell are described by the page, row, and column that contain the cell.

character variable
a variable whose values can consist of alphabetic and special characters as well as numeric characters.

correlation
the tendency for the values of a variable to become larger or smaller as the values of a variable increase or decrease.

correlation coefficient
a statistic, ranging from -1 to 1, measuring the strength of the linear relationship between two series of values.

critical value
the value of a statistic that corresponds to the desired significance level in a test of a hypothesis.

crossing
in the TABULATE procedure, the process that combines the effects of two or more elements.

crosstabulation table
a frequency table that displays the frequency distribution for two or more variables. These tables are often referred to as two-way, three-way, or n-way tables. See also frequency table.

DATA step
a group of statements in a SAS program that begins with a DATA statement and ends with either a RUN statement, another DATA statement, a PROC statement, the end of the job, or the semicolon that immediately follows instream data lines. The DATA step enables you to read raw data or other SAS data sets and use programming logic to create a SAS data set, write a report, or write to an external file.

database
an organized collection of related data.

degrees of freedom
a statistic that refers to the number of independent pieces of information contained in a sum.

descriptive statistic
a quantity that characterizes, rather than draws inference from, a collection of values. Types of descriptive statistics are measures of central tendency, measures of variation among values, and measures of the shape of the distribution of values.

descriptor information
(1) the information the SAS System creates and maintains identifying the attributes of a SAS data set and its contents.
(2) in the SAS data model, the logical component of a SAS data set that supplies the SAS System with information about the data set and its contents.

dimension expression
in the TABULATE procedure, the portion of the TABLE statement that defines what variables and statistics make up a single dimension of the table. The format of a dimension expression is the same for any of the three dimensions page, row, and column.

engine
a part of the SAS System that reads from or writes to a file. Each engine allows the SAS System to access files that have a particular format. There are several types of engines. See also interface view engine.

entry type
a characteristic of a SAS catalog entry that identifies its structure and attributes to the SAS System. When you create an entry, the SAS System automatically assigns the entry type as part of the name.

field
a window area that is defined to contain a value that users usually can view, enter, or modify.

format
a pattern that the SAS System uses to determine how a variable value should be displayed. The SAS System provides a set of standard formats and also enables you to define your own custom formats.

frequency table
a table that lists the values of a variable and the number of observations with each value. See also crosstabulation table.

informat

a pattern that the SAS System uses to determine how values entered in variable fields should be interpreted. The SAS System provides a set of standard informats and also enables you to define your own custom informats.

interface view engine

a SAS System engine that retrieves data directly from files that have been formatted by other software vendors.

libref

the name that is temporarily associated with a SAS data library. You assign a libref with a LIBNAME statement or with operating system control language.

logistic regression

a form of regression analysis in which the response variable represents a binary or ordinal-level response.

logit transformation

a natural log transformation of the probability, p, of the form $\log(p / (1 - p))$.

multiple linear regression

an analysis where a response variable is modeled as a linear combination of two or more explanatory factors.

normal distribution

an important theoretical probability distribution often used in both applied and theoretical statistics. The normal distribution has a bell-shaped probability density curve and is characterized by its mean (μ) and standard deviation (σ).

numeric variable

a variable that contains only numeric values and related symbols, such as decimal points, plus signs, and minus signs.

odds ratio

a measure of the degree of association between a predictor variable and an outcome variable when the data are collected retrospectively and summarized in 2 x 2 crosstabulation tables.

p-value

the observed significance level of a statistical test, representing the probability of observing a sample outcome more contradictory to the null hypothesis than the observed sample result. The smaller the p-value, the stronger the evidence for rejecting the null hypothesis. See also significance level.

regression analysis

an analysis of the nature of the relationship between two or more variables, expressed as a mathematical function. On a scatter plot, this relationship is diagrammed as a line drawn through data points. A straight line indicates simple regression; a curve indicates a higher-order regression.

regression equation

the mathematical equation expressing the expected value of the response variable as a function of the independent variables.

relative risk

a measure of the degree of association between a predictor variable and an outcome variable when the data are collected prospectively and summarized in 2 x 2 crosstabulation tables.

SAS catalog

a SAS file that stores many different kinds of information in smaller units called catalog entries. A single SAS catalog can contain several different types of catalog entries.

SAS catalog entry

a separate storage unit within a SAS catalog. Each entry has an entry type that identifies its structure to the SAS System. See also entry type.

SAS data set

descriptor information and its related data values organized as a table of observations and variables that can be processed by the SAS System. A SAS data set can be either a SAS data file or a SAS data view.

SAS data view

a SAS data set in which the descriptor information and the observations are obtained from other files. SAS data views store only the information required to retrieve data values or descriptor information.

SAS program

a group of SAS statements that guide the SAS System through a process or series of processes.

significance level

the probability of rejecting a true null hypothesis, that is, the probability of making a Type I error. See also *p*-value.

simple linear regression

an analysis where a response variable is modeled as a linear function of a single continuous explanatory factor, or independent variable. See also multiple linear regression.

stub-and-banner table

a report in which the rows, or stubs, of the table correspond to the levels of one or more nested variables and in which the columns, or banner, also correspond to the levels of one or more nested variables.

view descriptor

a SAS/ACCESS file that defines all or a subset of the DBMS data that are described by an access descriptor.

window

a visibly bounded area that displays text or graphical information or presents a space for you to communicate with a computer system.

Index

Special Characters

@ (at sign) column pointer control
   See column pointer control (@)
\# (pound sign) line pointer control
   See line pointer control (#)
/ (slash) line pointer control
   See line pointer control (/)

Your Turn

If you have comments or suggestions about *Introduction to Market Research Using the SAS System*, please send them to us on a photocopy of this page or send us electronic mail.

For comments about this book, please return the photocopy to

> SAS Institute Inc.
> Publications Division
> SAS Campus Drive
> Cary, NC 27513
> **email:** yourturn@unx.sas.com

For suggestions about the software, please return the photocopy to

> SAS Institute Inc.
> Technical Support Division
> SAS Campus Drive
> Cary, NC 27513
> **email:** suggest@unx.sas.com